5 00

Great Dinner Parties

Menus and Recipes for Dinners
for 4, 6, 8, 10, 12 and 16

by

BARBARA MYERS

Simon and Schuster
New York

Designed by Irving Perkins
Manufactured in the United States of America

1 2 3 4 5 6 7 8 9 10

Library of Congress Cataloging in Publication Data

Myers, Barbara.
Great dinner parties
Includes indexes.
1. Dinners and dining. 2. Menus. I. Title.
TX737.M9   641.5'4   75-14355
ISBN 0-671-22071-3

FOR MY DAUGHTER SYDNEY

Contents

NOTE

Dinner menus in this book for 4, 6 and 8 have been planned so that guests are seated and served. Menus for 10, 12 and 16 are intended as buffets.

How to Use This Book

About the Menus

There is a total of twenty-one dinner-party menus in this cookbook, ranging from those serving as few as four persons to those serving as many as sixteen. The menus, with accompanying recipes, are arranged in separate sections as follows (the page number refers to the beginning of each section).

Each recipe in a particular menu will serve the exact number of guests indicated. (If you expect to serve fourteen, use a menu for sixteen.) Main-course recipes are generous, allowing for second servings, but the first courses and dessert recipes (unless otherwise indicated) will provide only one serving per person.

Dinner menus for four, six and eight persons have been planned so that guests are seated and served the three courses at the dining-room table. All dinners for ten or more have been planned for buffet service, where the guests help themselves, then sit in the living room at individual tables or card tables. The appetizers, however, are to be served to the guests in the living room, and are the types of foods that go well with cocktails. In these buffet dinners the main course can be served on one plate—main dish, salad or vegetable and bread—with no cutting required. Desserts are also planned for living-room service. Coffee for all menus (unless otherwise indicated) may be served either with the dessert or separately.

Basic Lists and Preparation

To use this cookbook as it was intended, it will be helpful to follow this general procedure.

First decide whom you wish to invite and make out a guest list. Then extend the invitations, and when you know that everyone has accepted, turn to the section for serving that number of guests and select a menu.

Then make more lists. Look through the ingredients in each recipe and make a shopping list of those required. Be sure to check through your cupboards to make certain there is an adequate supply of sugar, flour, herbs and spices or other staples to carry you through. And don't forget to add coffee if needed—and cream or milk. Plan to replenish your stock of liquors, wines and liqueurs, if your party includes them. If you intend to use candles or flowers, add them to the list, along with a notation to have plenty of ice and cocktail napkins.

Then check through the recipes to see what serving equipment is required and, if you wish, jot down this information too. Plan a day when you can polish silver, copper or brass, and wash seldom-used crystal and serving dishes. If the party is large, it may be necessary to borrow or rent extra glasses, dishes and tableware; remember, too, to provide adequate seating and table space (card tables or individual tables are preferable to eating from your lap).

Several days before the party, purchase the staple items on your grocery list and any special or foreign ingredients. Leave the perishables such as fruits and some vegetables until a day or two before. (Breads, although perishable, freeze well, so they may be bought at any time that is convenient for you.)

As you planned your shopping, plan your tasks in the kitchen. First decide how you want to proceed. Look over the recipes and decide what you want to do one or two days before, what you will leave until the day of the party, and what must be done at the very end.

Take a look at the individual recipes again and prepare anything that can be done well in advance. Salad dressing, mayonnaise, bread crumbs, croutons, grated cheese, chopped nuts, chopped onions, hard-cooked eggs and clarified butter are in this category. The preparation of salad greens and some garnishes, even the partial precooking of vegetables, can be dealt with a day or two ahead.

With all of this basic beforehand work done, you will have paved the way for what I hope will be an enjoyable and relaxed few hours in the kitchen when you actually prepare the dinner.

Efficiency in the Kitchen

In preparing any dish, first read through the recipe so you have in mind the step-by-step preparation.

Bring ingredients such as cheese, butter and eggs to room temperature, if required (butter and cream cheese may take one to two hours to soften), along with the previously prepared "chopped, grated and toasted" ingredients. Then assemble the remaining ingredients (a tray is helpful for this) and necessary equipment, including paper towels, waxed paper and plastic wrap.

Look through the recipe and do any of the precooking, peeling, grating or chopping that you haven't done previously. Prepare the pans, molds or casseroles as required. Light the oven if necessary and set it to the correct temperature. Allow about ten minutes for the oven to reach the proper temperature.

At this point you are ready to begin. Follow the steps in the recipe in order given, setting aside each ingredient as it is used. Soak used utensils in warm soapy water. When you proceed in this manner, the preparation and cleanup are much easier and there is less opportunity for error.

For any dish that must be prepared or completed at the last minute, it will save time if you pre-measure ingredients (cooking-show style) and arrange them in the order of use at your working counter, or near the range. The French call this procedure *mise en place*.

As the day of the dinner party approaches, try to use up foods stored in the refrigerator so you can utilize it to best advantage. An empty shelf is handy. Line the shelf above with waxed paper to prevent anything dripping down and causing damage. Before the dinner guests arrive you may even want to arrange the appetizer or dessert on the individual plates and store them on this empty shelf. The freezing compartment is useful for storing extra ice cubes and breads or rolls you may have purchased days ahead.

Serving Foods Properly

Proper serving means essentially that hot foods should be served hot, and cold foods served cold. To ensure that hot foods stay hot, it is advisable to heat both the serving dishes and dinner plates. If you don't have a warming oven, warm plates a few minutes in the oven (as I do), unless your china is extremely fragile. For dinners of ten or more, when both main dish and salad are served on one plate, the plates should not be heated.

About the Ingredients

For perfect results when using the recipes in this cookbook, keep the following in mind.

MEASUREMENTS

All measurements are level.

Use standard-size measuring spoons, a glass liquid measure for liquid ingredients, and a set of dry measures for dry ingredients. Fill measuring spoons and dry-measure cups generously, then level off by cutting off the excess with a knife blade held at right angle. When measuring dried and fresh herbs, press lightly with the flat of the blade to level.

FLOUR

All-purpose flour should be sifted directly into the measuring cup, then leveled off. If pre-sifted flour is used, it should be sifted again. The recipes were tested with unbleached flour.

SUGAR

White granulated sugar is used in all recipes requiring sugar, unless otherwise specified. Superfine is suggested for several dessert recipes because it dissolves more quickly.

Confectioners' sugar should be sifted before using, as should cornstarch.

EGGS AND DAIRY PRODUCTS

Large eggs are used whenever eggs are called for, unless otherwise indicated.

Butter used is lightly salted unless sweet butter (unsalted) or clarified butter is specified. (For a recipe for clarified butter consult Index II: Basic Recipes and Techniques.)

Lightly whipped cream means heavy cream that has been whipped until it barely holds its shape. This is preferred as a garnish for desserts and usually for molds with gelatin, as it produces a light, velvety-textured dish. Stiffly beaten cream should be whipped until it will hold a peak: it should be stiff but not buttery. This is the preferred method for whipped-cream fillings. To whip cream properly, chill the bowl and beaters.

Sour cream is dairy sour cream, not fresh cream that has been soured. A special aged cream called Crème Fraîche is used in several recipes. (Consult Index II: Basic Recipes and Techniques.)

Cheese is natural, not processed, cheese.

OILS AND SHORTENINGS

Olive oil for salad dressings should, in general, be that imported from France or Italy. Spanish and Greek olive oils are heavier and stronger-flavored, but can be used with careful tasting. They are excellent for sautéed foods.

Peanut oil is required in some recipes; it is favored by the French for salad dressings and by the Chinese for frying. It has a delicate flavor and does not absorb cooking flavors. Corn oil is also good for deep frying.

Vegetable oil refers to any bland vegetable oil—specifically not aromatic olive oil. (You may think of it as salad oil.)

Vegetable shortening means Spry, Crisco, Fluffo or similar products.

VINEGAR

Red wine vinegar is specified in some salad dressings because it has more flavor than distilled white vinegar and is less harsh than cider vinegar.

AROMATICS, HERBS AND SPICES

Garlic cloves should be peeled before putting through a garlic press. To crush with the flat blade of a knife, place a heavy knife blade over the unpeeled clove and pound lightly with your fist to barely split the garlic clove, not to mash it. Then remove peel.

Chopped parsley means fresh parsley. The dried has little flavor. There are 2 varieties: curly (the most familiar) and flat-leaf Italian (which has a more decided flavor). Use curly unless otherwise indicated.

Dried herbs should be fragrant. If yours have a musty odor, discard them and buy new ones. Crush dried herbs in the palm of one hand with your other palm before using, to release the oils.

Whole spices are preferred, when available, as ground ones lose strength after a period of time.

Freshly grated nutmeg refers to nutmeg grated from a whole nutmeg on the finest blade of the grater. The powdered nutmeg has little flavor.

Coarse salt is large-crystal salt, labeled and sold as kosher salt. I feel it has more flavor.

Pepper should be freshly ground in a pepper mill for greater pungency.

All flavoring extracts should be labeled "pure," not "imitation."

Flavoring extracts and some wines, brandies and liqueurs are added to hot sauces after they have cooled a few minutes because part of the essence cooks away if the mixture is too hot.

WINES AND CHICKEN BROTH

Wines used in cooking are table wines (the kind you would like to drink), not so-called "cooking" wines.

Rich chicken broth is either a flavorful homemade one or one canned with a little chicken fat, not the kind made with hot water and bouillon cubes or granules.

The Indexes

There are three indexes: Index I is a general index; Index II, basic recipes and techniques; and Index III, foreign and American regional recipes.

Index I: General Index page 237

A bullet (·) in front of many of the recipes indicates that these are Quick and Easy: that is, they take little preparation or can be prepared at the last minute (sometimes both). This is a valuable group; it is one to keep in mind when preparation time is at a minimum and substitute dishes are necessary.

Index II: Basic Recipes and Techniques page 253

This group includes a few basic recipes or "how to" techniques that are required in more than one recipe in the cookbook. In the recipes they are indicated by "See Index II." All other basic recipes and techniques are given in the text along with the individual recipes.

Index III: Foreign and American Regional Recipes page 254

Since the cookbook relies heavily on ethnic recipes, I felt a separate index of these might be an interesting addition. All of these recipes are also listed in Index I.

MENUS
AND
RECIPES

Menus and Recipes
for Four

MENU

Chilled Polish Cream of Mushroom Soup

This is a properly made cream soup, not one of those woeful ones made with milk and thickened with flour. It has a flavorful broth base and is enriched with pure cream. The caraway seeds give this mushroom soup a haunting flavor.

Must be prepared in advance.

- 1½ tablespoons butter
- ¼ pound fresh mushrooms, coarsely chopped (buy those with gills showing for more flavor)
- 1 small onion, coarsely chopped (¼ cup)
- 1¾ cups rich chicken broth (canned if preferred)
- ¼ teaspoon paprika
- ¼ teaspoon caraway seeds
- ¼ cup Crème Fraîche (see Index II)
- Salt to taste

GARNISH:
Crème Fraîche (about 4 tablespoons)
Fresh dill (4 sprigs)
Paprika

1. Heat a 2-quart, heavy saucepan; then add the butter. When hot, add mushrooms and sauté over medium-high heat, stirring, until lightly browned, about 5 minutes (to give the soup color as well as added flavor). Add the onions and stir 2 to 3 minutes, but do not brown.

2. Add the chicken broth, paprika and caraway seeds. Simmer, covered, for 15 minutes. Remove from heat and cool slightly.

3. Pour into a blender and purée on low a few seconds. Don't overblend, as you want some texture. Stir in the ¼ cup Crème Fraîche. Add salt to taste. Chill in refrigerator until ready to serve, overnight if desired.

PRESENTATION: Stir to blend, taste and add more salt if necessary (cold soups often need more salt than those served hot). Ladle into small bowls (servings will be small) and float a dollop of Crème Fraîche on each; sprinkle with paprika and garnish with a sprig of dill.

Duckling au Poivre

This recipe is a double gift. First, real French flavor; second, ease in carving. Pounded peppercorns and a cognac sauce are the basics of a traditional French steak au poivre. Borrowing that idea, I found that roast duck also takes well to the same pungent treatment. Carving a roast duckling is usually difficult because there is so little flesh on the bones. This method simplifies the procedure. The breast, instead of being thinly sliced from the bone, is cut away in sections. Each person is served part of the breast, and either a leg or thigh. The wings are saved for second servings, but may not be needed because the duck is rich.

May be partially prepared in advance.

1 tablespoon whole peppercorns
1 Long Island duckling (4½ to 5 pounds)
  Salt

1 onion, unpeeled and cut in half
  Vegetable oil
¼ cup cognac or other brandy
4 tablespoons softened butter

GARNISH:
Sprigs of watercress

1. Coarsely crush the peppercorns with a mortar and pestle, or crush them on a flat surface with the bottom of a heavy skillet or bottom of a bottle. They must not be too fine.

2. Rinse duckling and dry. Cut off excess neck skin; fasten remainder with a skewer. Prick fatty parts at ½-inch intervals to allow the fat to escape and skin to become crisp when roasting. Pull out excess fat from the cavity; sprinkle inside lightly with salt and insert onion halves. Brush lightly with oil. Press crushed peppercorns onto outside skin with the heel of the hand, covering just the breast, legs and thighs. Sprinkle lightly with salt. Cover loosely with waxed paper and refrigerate overnight. Before roasting, remove from refrigerator and bring to room temperature for accurate timing.

3. Meanwhile, rinse neck, liver, gizzard and heart and put in a saucepan with water to cover; add ¼ teaspoon salt. Bring to a boil, skim, then reduce heat and simmer 1 hour. Strain and discard neck and giblets. Reserve the broth. You will need ½ cup; if you have more than ½ cup, boil rapidly to reduce; if less, add water.

4. To roast the duckling, place on a rack in an open roasting pan, breast side up. Do not truss or cover. Roast in a preheated 325° oven for 1 hour and 20 minutes for the smaller duckling; 10 minutes longer for the larger one. Turn oven up to 425°, prick skin again, and roast about 15 to 20 minutes longer. It is not necessary to baste. The fat will pour out and the skin will become nicely browned and crisp. To tell if the bird is done, prick the thickest part of the thigh deeply with a fork. The juices should run clear. Remove from the oven, place on a heated platter and let stand in a warm place while making the sauce.

5. To make the sauce, pour off fat from roasting pan, leaving

about 1 tablespoon. Add the reserved ½ cup stock and boil down rapidly over high heat, scraping browned bits from pan. Reduce to about half. Then add the cognac and boil rapidly a minute or two to evaporate the alcohol. Off heat swirl in the butter, a tablespoon at a time. Taste and correct seasoning. Do not strain. Pour into a small warm sauceboat.

PRESENTATION: Garnish duckling platter with watercress, and carve as suggested below.

To prepare in advance: Complete steps 1 through 3, up to roasting the duckling.

Carving a Duckling for 4: With the legs toward the carver, cut off wings and reserve for second servings. Cut off legs and thighs in one piece, then separate at the joint. Cut straight down on one side of the breastbone, so close to the bone that the knife almost scrapes it; then turn knife outward to remove whole breast section. Repeat on the opposite side and cut each breast section in 2 pieces. Serve each person a piece of breast meat and either a leg or thigh, spooning the sauce over all as served. (It is rich and a spoonful is sufficient.)

Hot Fresh Tomatoes

This is a method rather than a recipe, so you may use any number of tomatoes. It is one of the best ways to serve those perfectly shaped "tomatoes in a tube" available the year round in supermarkets. These are rather tasteless and heating tends to improve their flavor.

May be partially prepared in advance.

> 4 to 6 small tomatoes (about 2 inches in diameter)
> Vegetable oil
> Salt

1. With a very sharp knife score each tomato twice vertically through the stem end, cutting just through the skin, barely into the flesh. Do not remove the core.

2. Rub the tomatoes with the oil and place, core side down, in an oiled, shallow baking dish; the tomatoes should not touch each other or the edge of the pan.

3. Bake in a preheated 425° oven for 8 to 10 minutes, or until very hot and skins start to pull away.

4. Remove from oven and peel away the skins as you carefully transfer them to a warm serving platter, or return to baking dish if this is attractive enough for serving. Leave cores intact; they are to be cut away when eating.

PRESENTATION: Salt lightly and serve hot without garnish. The beauty is the simplicity here.

To prepare in advance: Complete steps 1 and 2, up to baking.

Gratin Dauphinois

This is a French potato dish of humble origins in the mountainous province of Dauphiné. The ingredients are few; the result is delicious.

May be partially prepared in advance.

- 1¼ pounds (4 medium) baking potatoes (Idaho preferred)
- ½ clove garlic
- 2 tablespoons soft butter
- 1 teaspoon salt
- ⅛ teaspoon freshly ground pepper
- 2 ounces coarsely grated Gruyère cheese (about ½ cup)
- ¾ cup milk

1. Peel potatoes and drop into cold salted water (1 teaspoon salt to 1 quart water). Then cut lengthwise in halves or quarters and slice ⅛ inch thick; return to the cold water. Leave until ready to use. (You should have 3 cups.)

2. Rub a shallow flameproof baking dish* (1 quart) with the cut clove of garlic; discard garlic. Spread the dish with 1 tablespoon of the soft butter.

3. Drain the potatoes well in a colander but do not dry. Spread half in the prepared baking dish. Dot with ½ tablespoon butter and sprinkle with half the salt, pepper and grated Gruyère cheese in order named. Make another layer of potatoes, using the remaining ½ tablespoon butter and the rest of the salt, pepper and cheese.

4. Add the milk and place baking dish directly over medium heat until bubbles appear around the edge (do not boil). Then place in upper third of a preheated 425° oven about 20 minutes, or until potatoes are tender, milk has been absorbed and top is golden.

> PRESENTATION: Bring the baking dish directly to the table. No garnish is necessary.

To prepare in advance: Complete steps 1 and 2, up to "building" the casserole. It cannot be assembled ahead as the potatoes will discolor.

A delicious variation: Proceed as above but beat 1 large egg until frothy, increase milk to 1 cup and combine. Pour over potatoes, bring just to a simmer and bake in upper third of a 350° oven for about 30 minutes.

Celery Leaf Salad

Here is a marinated salad that somehow retains a crisp, fresh flavor. The top halves only of two bunches of celery are used

---

* This must be baked in a container that can be brought to the table. An enameled skillet is ideal, providing the handle (if wooden or plastic) can be removed. The container must be shallow for quick—and proper—baking.

because this is mainly a celery *leaf* salad. (The celery flavor is all at the top.) For family, use one whole bunch; it is second best but still excellent.

Should be prepared in advance.

2 bunches Pascal celery, the top half only, to make 1
  quart sliced celery tops
1 tablespoon red wine vinegar
2 tablespoons fresh lemon juice
½ teaspoon grated lemon zest*
1 teaspoon dry mustard
1½ teaspoons celery seed (optional)†
⅛ teaspoon monosodium glutamate
1½ teaspoons salt
8 tablespoons olive oil

1. Unless the celery is dirty, do not wash, but cut off dried ends and remove any bruised leaves. If necessary, separate stalks and rinse, but dry thoroughly and re-form to appoximate the original bunches.

2. Cut across the ribs from the leaf end in fine slices (¼ inch or less), leaves and all, using enough of the celery to provide 1 quart.

3. Pour the vinegar and lemon juice into a bowl large enough to accommodate the celery. Add the grated lemon zest, mustard, celery seed, monosodium glutamate and salt; beat with a fork to blend. Then gradually beat in the olive oil.

4. Add the celery to the marinade and mix well. Let stand in a cool place at least 1 hour, mixing once or twice. If kept longer (up to 4 hours) refrigerate, but remove ½ hour before serving. It should be cool and crisp, not icy cold.

PRESENTATION: Spoon onto small individual salad plates. No garnish is necessary as the leaves provide a contrast in shades of green.

* Lemon zest is only the yellow part of the peel, with none of the white.
† The celery seed may be omitted, but it gives a slight, attractive bitterness.

Strawberries in Sauce Sabayon

These are fresh strawberries in a velvety wine sauce. Hot saba-yon must be made and served immediately. This cold version has the addition of whipped cream and may be made a day in advance. The sabayon recipe is from the Restaurant Chantraine in Brussels, the cold version with strawberries my own invention.
Must be prepared in advance.

> 1 pint strawberries
> Sauce Sabayon (recipe below)

Rinse the strawberries quickly, hull and dry on paper toweling. Chill until ready to serve.

> PRESENTATION: Spoon Sauce Sabayon into 4 large wineglasses. Arrange strawberries on top. Serve chilled.

SAUCE SABAYON

> 2 egg yolks
> 5 teaspoons sugar
> 1½ tablespoons port wine
> 1½ tablespoons dry white wine
> ½ cup heavy cream, whipped until stiff but not buttery

1. Beat the egg yolks slightly in a large round-bottom mixing bowl. Add the sugar and the port and white wines. Whip until frothy, using a wire whisk. Then place in a skillet of simmering water set over very low heat. Tip the bowl and whip vigorously until the mixture swells into a thick golden foam and there is no layer of unbeaten egg at the bottom. It should mound lightly. (Do not overcook or the sabayon will deflate.)

2. Immediately remove from heat and place in a bowl of ice water (with cubes). Whip until cool. Then fold in the whipped cream. Refrigerate, covered, until ready to serve.

Note: This sauce may be made a day in advance.

MENU

Indian Samosas

Samosas are triangular fried pastries made and sold in all parts of India. This particular recipe is Indian but comes by way of East Africa where there is a large Indian population. Sometimes the crisp wrapping encloses a vegetable filling, sometimes meat. In this version, a spicy meat filling is used. The recipe is lengthy, the procedure of wrapping and filling is tedious, but the effort is rewarded with an unusual and tasty appetizer.

May be prepared in advance.

> 1 cup unsifted all-purpose flour (plus extra flour in a sieve for dusting pastries)
> ¼ teaspoon salt
> ½ teaspoon oil (plus extra for brushing pastries)
> Water (about 6 to 7 tablespoons)
> Meat filling (recipe below)
> Oil for deep frying
>
> GARNISH:
> 2 limes, cut in quarters

34

1. Mix the flour and salt together in a mixing bowl. Stir in the ½ teaspoon oil and enough water to make a soft dough that can be kneaded and rolled (about 6 to 7 tablespoons).

2. Knead thoroughly, at least 5 minutes, until the dough is very smooth and elastic. Divide into 4 equal portions. Cover with inverted mixing bowl and let stand 1 hour for easier rolling.

Note: To measure accurately, with hands roll dough into a 6-inch cylinder, then cut in four 1½-inch lengths.

3. Take 2 portions and roll out each separately into a 4-inch circle. Brush each lightly with oil and dust over lightly with the flour you have put in a sieve. Place 1 circle on top of the other, oiled and floured sides facing, and roll out into a large circle at least 9 inches in diameter. It must be very thin.

Note: So that both sides will be the same size, you will need to turn the pastry over several times while rolling out.

4. Repeat preceding process with remaining 2 portions of dough. You now have two 9-inch circles of pastry.

5. One at a time, place in a dry hot skillet or on a griddle for 10 to 15 seconds; turn and bake on other side for a few seconds longer. Do not brown or let dry. When ready to remove, air bubbles will begin to show in the pastry on the underside. Remove from heat, let cool a moment and carefully peel the 2 rounds apart. Repeat with remaining circle of pastry. Place under a clean towel to prevent drying out and proceed with next step.

6. Cut 1 pastry round into 3 equal strips. To form samosas, first prepare a thickish paste with 1 tablespoon flour and about 2 teaspoons water. Then take 1 strip of pastry and place short side toward you; fold edge of pastry over so that the bottom edge meets a side edge and forms a triangle. Seal the side edges with some of the flour paste and fill the pocket thus formed with a tablespoon of the meat mixture. Continue folding over from side to side to end of strip, and seal top edge with more flour paste—also any exposed corners that may allow the filling to escape during frying.

Note: The rounded strips will be a little more difficult to do but the end result will be the same. The first fold should be toward the curved edge.

7. Repeat above procedure with remaining pastry. You will then have 12 filled samosas.

8. To fry, heat at least 3 inches of oil in a deep-fat fryer to 375°. Fry only 4 to 6 samosas at a time for 3 to 5 minutes, or until golden brown and pastry is cooked through and crisp. Turn with tongs to brown both sides evenly. Drain on paper toweling and keep warm in a 200° oven while frying remainder. Yield: 12 samosas.

> PRESENTATION: Serve while warm, 3 to a person, with a wedge of lime to be squeezed over each bite. These are to be picked up and eaten with the fingers. They may be arranged on individual plates, or passed on a serving platter.

To prepare in advance: Complete all steps through deep-fat frying; cool and let stand at room temperature until ready to serve, then reheat in a 375° oven until hot, about 5 minutes.

Note: The unfried pastries may be made a day ahead and stored, covered, in the refrigerator with waxed paper between layers. Bring to room temperature before frying. The filling may be prepared 2 days in advance.

Meat Filling

    ¼ pound ground lamb or beef (½ cup)
    4 cloves garlic, put through a press
    1 teaspoon oil
    ½ teaspoon salt
    1 medium onion, finely chopped (½ cup)
    2 small green chilies, seeded and chopped*
    ¼ cup chopped fresh coriander leaves†

* Substitute canned Mexican jalapeño peppers if the fresh are not available.
† Fresh coriander is also known as *culantro, cilantro* or Chinese parsley, and as *dhania* in India. It can be found in Spanish or Chinese markets as it is widely used by these cultures. It is a pungent herb resembling parsley in appearance but not in taste; it has no flavor substitute. In this recipe use chopped parsley for color if coriander is not available. The flavor, of course, will be a little different.

¼ teaspoon ground cloves
¼ teaspoon ground cinnamon
¼ teaspoon ground cumin or crushed cumin seeds

1. Sauté the meat and garlic in the oil until meat is dry, using a fork to break up fine. Remove from heat and drain off fat.
2. Add the salt, chopped onion, chopped chilies, coriander, cloves, cinnamon and cumin; mix well. Do not cook further. Set aside to cool.

Chicken Tandoori

In India, chicken seasoned and marinated in this manner—in spices and yogurt—is baked on iron skewers in a clay charcoal oven called a *tandoor*. This version approximates one served at the Three Bells, an Asian restaurant in Nairobi, Kenya. The chicken is roasted in a substitute American oven, then carved and served in its spicy marinade, which is the color of melted gold. Not quite authentic, but superb.

Must be partially prepared in advance.

A 4- to 4½-pound roasting chicken
Juice of 1 lemon (2 tablespoons)
2 teaspoons salt
1 teaspoon cumin seed
1 teaspoon coriander seed
1 teaspoon crushed dried red pepper
1 large onion
6 cloves garlic
Peeled fresh ginger (1-inch piece)
2 teaspoons turmeric
½ cup vegetable oil
1 tablespoon vinegar
1 cup yogurt

GARNISH:
Sprigs of fresh coriander or parsley

1. Rinse the chicken and dry; remove any fat from the cavity. With a small, sharp knife, cut 3 diagonal 2-inch slits on each side of the breast, about ½ inch deep. Make 2 similar cuts each in the legs and thighs. Combine the salt with the lemon juice and rub this mixture into the slits and over the rest of the chicken. Put the chicken in a deep bowl (nonmetallic) for marinating and set aside.

2. To make the marinade, grind the cumin seed, coriander seed, and crushed dried red pepper in a mortar until fine. Chop the onion, garlic and ginger separately; then chop together until fine. Place in a small bowl and add the ground spice mixture and turmeric. Stir in the oil, vinegar and then the yogurt.

Note: If preferred, put all ingredients except the yogurt in a blender and blend until onion and garlic are finely chopped; then add yogurt and blend to mix.

3. Pour marinade over the chicken, turning to coat all surfaces. Then cover and refrigerate overnight, or leave at room temperature at least 4 hours. Turn occasionally during the marinating period. Bring to room temperature, if refrigerated, when ready to roast. Do not truss.

4. To roast, place the chicken on its side (no rack) in a well-buttered shallow roasting pan just large enough to hold the chicken. (This is important because the marinade may dry out and burn if the pan is too large. An oval baking dish is perfect.) Pour the marinade over the chicken. Do not cover.

5. Place in the lower third of a preheated 375° oven. Roast for 30 minutes, basting once or twice with the marinade. Turn on other side and roast 30 minutes, again basting twice. Then turn breast up, lower the heat to 350° and roast for 20 to 30 minutes longer. Test for doneness by cutting into the thigh at the joint. Juices should run clear. The chicken will be charred attractively in places.

6. Remove from oven and place on a heated platter. Spoon off the fat from the marinade and pour the marinade into a warm sauceboat to be served with the chicken.

PRESENTATION: Garnish the platter with sprigs of fresh coriander or parsley. Carve as for any roasting chicken, but spoon sauce over portions as served, and the rice suggested in this menu.

To prepare in advance: Complete steps 1 through 3, up to roasting. If desired, the roasted chicken may be held in a warm oven up to ½ hour before serving. To do this, remove chicken and turn oven down to 200°, leaving oven door partially open to cool rapidly. When the proper temperature is reached, return chicken to oven.

Steamed Basmati Rice

Basmati is a long-grain white rice that comes from the northern part of India. It is aged and has a slightly toasted flavor. Any long-grain white rice may be substituted in this recipe, but it must be the nonconverted type, like Carolina rice.

May be prepared in advance.

   1 cup Basmati rice,* or long-grain rice (not converted)
   1 cup cold water
   1 teaspoon salt

1. Measure rice and put into a 2-quart heavy saucepan. Pick over and remove any brown grains with hulls. Wash, rubbing the rice through your fingers in several changes of water until the water is almost clear. (This rids the rice of excess starch and prevents scorching when cooking.) Cover with water and let stand 1 hour, then drain off water. (If Carolina type rice is used, there is no need to soak.)
2. Add cold water equal in amount to rice (for this recipe 1 cup); stir in salt, then level the rice with your hand. Bring to a

* Basmati rice is available in 1-pound boxes in foreign food stores or in stores specializing in Indian foods. Rajah brand is a good one.

boil over high heat, then cover and reduce heat to as low as possible. Let the rice steam for 13 to 15 minutes. Do not remove lid during this period. Rice is done when water is absorbed and rice is dry. (At the minimum time, tip pan to see if any water is remaining; if so, cook a minute or two longer.) Remove pan from heat, and let stand, covered, 15 minutes longer to complete the steaming process.

3. After this second steaming period, remove lid and stir the rice with a fork to fluff and separate the grains. It may be kept covered in a 200° oven up to ½ hour. Yield: 3 cups.

PRESENTATION: Serve in a heated bowl.

To prepare in advance: Complete step 1 a few hours in advance; be sure to drain rice. Or, steam, stir and cool uncovered. To reheat, sprinkle with 2 teaspoons of water, stir, cover and reheat in a 350° oven 10 to 15 minutes.

Avocado and Spanish Onions

The idea for this salad, which is simplicity itself, comes from Peru, where avocados and sweet red onions are abundant.
May be partially prepared in advance.

> 1 medium, sweet red onion (Spanish, Bermuda or Italian), chopped (½ cup)
> ¼ cup olive oil
> 1½ tablespoons red wine vinegar
> ½ teaspoon salt
> 2 medium avocados (firm but ripe)

> GARNISH:
> Chopped parsley

1. To make the dressing, combine the chopped onion, oil, vinegar and salt.

2. Cut avocados in half lengthwise and remove pits. Peel the avocados and place cavity side down. Cut lengthwise in ¼-inch slices and place in a shallow bowl.

3. Immediately pour dressing over avocado slices to prevent discoloring. Carefully lift slices with a spatula and tip bowl to let dressing seep in between. Do not let stand more than a few minutes.

PRESENTATION: Arrange avocado slices, fanshaped, on individual salad plates. Pour dressing on top. Garnish each plate with a sprinkling of chopped parsley. Serve immediately.

To prepare in advance: Make dressing as in step 1 a few hours in advance. The avocados must be sliced at the last minute as they will discolor even in the dressing if allowed to stand any length of time.

Fresh Mangoes, a Unique Way of Serving

Fresh mangoes are the preferred dessert, but since they are seasonal (and never available in some parts of the country) I have included as an alternative an American dessert which is made from typically Indian ingredients—oranges and coconut. The mangoes here are served in the skin, cut to remove the large flat seed, then scored and pressed from underneath to raise the cubes of sweet yellow or orange flesh for attractive serving and easy eating. This is an idea from coastal East Africa, where excellent mangoes are grown.

May be prepared in advance.

2 ripe, medium mangoes, about 1 pound each*

GARNISH:
4 sprigs of mint

---

* Mangoes are ripe when part of the green skin has turned orange or red, depending on variety, and when they feel slightly soft. Your produce man can help you here. Store in the refrigerator when ripe, to stop the ripening process.

1. Cut a thin sliver off the ends of the mangoes. (This will help them to stand properly when served.) To remove the seed, stand one mango on end, pointed end up. Cut down through the center until you feel the large flattish seed; cut close to it and down through the other end. Then repeat with other half to free the seed; discard. Repeat with remaining mango.

2. Cut through the flesh (not the skin) lengthwise, using a table knife, then crosswise to make ¾-inch sections. Cover with plastic wrap. Chill. The mangoes will not discolor.

PRESENTATION: Carefully push up the skin from underneath to raise and spread the flesh to form cubes. Place half a mango on each dessert plate and garnish with a sprig of mint. Provide teaspoons for eating.

Note: Although preparing a mango in this manner is easy (once you have tried it), you may wish to purchase an extra mango for practice. (It is a delicious breakfast fruit.) If the finished mango halves are not attractive, simply cut away the cubes from the skins and serve in stemmed wineglasses. You will have lost none of the flavor, only the unique method of cutting and serving.

Ambrosia

Straight from the South, this fruit dessert is often made with the addition of bananas and pineapple, but I prefer this simple version. I often serve it as an appetizer for brunch.
Must be prepared in advance.

    4 thick-skinned seedless oranges (Jaffa from Israel preferred, or Sunkist)
    1 cup moist shredded coconut*
    2 tablespoons sugar (more if oranges are tart)

* I use Baker's Angel Flake Coconut.

1. Peel oranges, removing all of the spongy white. Cut in half from blossom end, then slice ¼ inch thick.

2. Arrange a layer of oranges in a glass serving bowl, sprinkle with a little of the sugar, then add a layer of coconut. Repeat layers ending with coconut. Cover and chill at least 1 hour, but overnight if preferred.

PRESENTATION: Bring fruit bowl directly from the refrigerator to the table. It must be cold. It looks best served on individual dessert plates. You will need forks here.

MENU

FIRST COURSE: *Iced Mussels Ravigote*

MAIN COURSE: • *London Broil, Charcoal Grilled*
                • *Cherry Tomatoes Provençale*
                Hashed Brown Potatoes
                • *French Bread with Black Butter*

DESSERT: • *Poached Fresh Peaches and Cream*
             Coffee

             • Quick and Easy Recipe

Iced Mussels Ravigote

Respected by the French, adored by the Belgians, this delicious shellfish is virtually neglected in the United States. Yet it is commercially gathered along both the Atlantic and Pacific coasts. Mussel shells are either dark brown or blue-black and make attractive serving receptacles for the orange flesh, which has a sweet and subtle flavor. Here the morsels are served on the half shell, nestled in crushed ice, and buried under an herb sauce which complements their delicacy.
Must be prepared in advance.

24 large fresh mussels (6 per person; 8 to 10 if mussels
      are small), cleaned (method below)
½ cup water
¼ cup vinegar
      Crushed ice
      Ravigote Sauce (recipe below)

GARNISH:
Chopped parsley
Lemon slices

44

1. Place cleaned mussels in a large saucepan; add water and vinegar. Cover, bring to a boil and steam open. (This will take 3 to 5 minutes.) Remove from heat and cool slightly. Discard any mussels that have not opened.

2. When cool enough to handle, remove mussels from shells. Chill covered. Separate shells and reserve the largest halves, discarding the rest.

3. On 4 chilled salad plates, spread a bed of crushed ice; nestle 6 half shells, spoke style, on top of each (points inward). Place in freezer until ready to serve (plates may be stacked), or if no freezer space is available, arrange just before serving.

> PRESENTATION: Place a mussel in each half shell and top with a spoonful of Ravigote Sauce. Decorate with a sprinkle of chopped parsley. Cut 4 lemon slices to the center once, twist and stand one in the center of each plate. You will need cocktail forks for this.

To prepare in advance: Complete all steps, up to Presentation, and make Ravigote Sauce—all the day before if desired.

RAVIGOTE SAUCE

　　　　1 large, fresh egg yolk
　　　　1 hard-cooked egg
　　　1/8 teaspoon dry mustard
　　　　　Pinch of sugar
　　　1/2 teaspoon finely minced scallion
　　　1/2 teaspoon finely minced shallot
　　　1/2 teaspoon finely minced parsley
　　　1/2 teaspoon finely minced chives
　　　1/3 cup mayonnaise
　　　1/4 teaspoon salt (or to taste)

Beat egg yolk slightly. Cut the hard-cooked egg in quarters and press through a sieve into the yolk, add the mustard, sugar, minced scallion, shallot, parsley and chives. Fold in the mayonnaise. Add salt to taste. Chill several hours to blend flavors.

To clean mussels: Scrape off barnacles with a knife; pull off the beards; scrub shells clean under running water. Drain and store in the refrigerator for a day or two, if desired, before cooking. Mussels rarely contain sand, so it is not necessary to soak them in water.

London Broil, Charcoal Grilled

Flank steak is not a tender cut of beef, but grilled rare and carved in this manner, it can hold its own among sirloins or porterhouse steaks of better basic quality. If you like your meats charcoal flavored, this is for you.

A beef flank steak (1½ to 1¾ pounds)
Salt
Freshly ground pepper
4   tablespoons melted butter
½   teaspoon Worcestershire sauce

GARNISH:
1 tablespoon chopped chives, fresh or
   frozen

1. Remove any tough membrane from edge of steak; dry and refrigerate until ready to broil. Contrary to the usual rule, this steak must be grilled when cold, so remove it from the refrigerator at the last minute.

2. To charcoal-grill, be certain the coals are at maximum heat. The rack should be placed 1½ to 2 inches above the coals and preheated. Brush the rack with oil, then put the cold steak on the hot rack and broil 3 minutes on the first side. Turn and broil 3 to 5 minutes on second side. It should be well seared but not cooked through, as it must be rare to be tender.

PRESENTATION: Place on a heated serving platter. Season with salt and pepper to taste; pour the melted butter over and sprinkle with the Worcestershire sauce.

Sprinkle chopped chives over the top. Serve immediately without additional garnish, which might interfere with the carving technique.

To carve: With a sharp knife held almost parallel to the platter, carve the meat across the grain into very thin slices, about ¼ inch thick. This cuts across the tough fibers, helping to tenderize the meat. The meat juices will blend with the seasoned melted butter, providing a simple sauce. Spoon this sauce over each portion as served.

Cherry Tomatoes Provençale

Tiny tomatoes sautéed in garlic oil—what could be simpler; more delicious?
May be partially prepared in advance.

> 1 pint carton cherry tomatoes (or at least 24)
> 3 tablespoons olive oil
> ½ clove garlic, crushed with flat of a knife
> Salt to taste
> Freshly ground pepper to taste

1. Wash and stem tomatoes; roll on paper toweling to dry.
2. Heat olive oil in a skillet large enough to accommodate the tomatoes in a single layer. Add garlic and cook briefly to extract the flavor. When garlic is golden, remove it and discard. (Do not allow it to burn or it will turn the oil bitter.)
3. Add tomatoes to oil and sauté over medium heat a few minutes, shaking pan occasionally. The skins will begin to split when sizzling hot. Remove immediately from heat and season to taste with salt and pepper.

PRESENTATION: Serve while hot in any type of serving dish. No garnish is necessary since the tomatoes themselves are a garnish.

To prepare in advance: Complete steps 1 and 2, up to sautéing the tomatoes. Reheat the oil when ready to sauté.

Hashed Brown Potatoes

A combination of bacon drippings, butter and grated onion make these the best hashed brown potatoes I have eaten. Directions must be followed exactly. The mealy quality of the Idaho baker is required; do not substitute another variety.

Must be partially prepared in advance.

4   medium Idaho baking potatoes (1 ¼ pounds)
1   tablespoon finely grated onion
1   teaspoon salt
¼   teaspoon freshly ground pepper
3   tablespoons bacon drippings
3   tablespoons butter

1. Bake the potatoes in a preheated 400° oven just until soft, about 45 minutes. (Do not overbake.) Remove to a cooling rack; cut a gash in each to allow the steam to escape. When cool, refrigerate overnight. (They must be cold.)

2. Peel cold potatoes, leaving any lightly browned underskin attached. Grate onto a sheet of waxed paper, using a medium blade. There should be 4 cups. Sprinkle onion, salt and pepper over the top and toss gently to distribute seasonings.

3. Melt bacon drippings in a heavy 9-inch skillet over medium-high heat. When hot, drop grated potatoes in by the handful over the entire surface; level but do not pack down. Dot the top with small chunks of the butter. Turn heat down to medium and sauté, without stirring, until crisp and brown on the underside, about 15 minutes. Break up slightly with a spatula and turn potatoes over in sections. Lightly brown on the other side, about 5 minutes.

Note: If the potatoes are sautéed too slowly, they will steam and turn soggy.

PRESENTATION: Turn out onto a heated serving plate, top side up, arranging the potatoes in the same round shape.

To prepare in advance: Complete steps 1 and 2, up to sautéing, but refrigerate again, as the potatoes should be cold to cook properly.

French Bread with Black Butter

Butter simmered long enough to turn a golden-brown color (not actually black) also takes on a hazelnut flavor and gives a new dimension to hot French bread.
May be partially prepared in advance.

¼ pound butter
1 long loaf (8 to 10 ounces) French bread, split hori
    zontally lengthwise

1. Melt the butter in a 2-quart heavy saucepan over low heat, then shake the pan until the moisture has cooked away and the butter begins to turn brown. At first it will bubble up and crackle, then subside just before turning color.
2. Using a pastry brush, spread butter over cut sides of bread and crust. Re-form the loaf.
3. Wrap in aluminum foil with the opening at the top; store at room temperature or freeze.
4. When ready to serve, open the foil and bake in a preheated 350° oven for 10 minutes; if frozen, bake without thawing for 15 minutes, or until it is heated through and crust is crisp.

PRESENTATION: Cut through in 3-inch diagonal slices. Re-form in long French-bread basket, or separate the slices and arrange buttered side up in any type basket.

To prepare in advance: Complete steps 1 through 3, up to heating.

Poached Fresh Peaches and Cream

Poached fresh peaches with 3 delicate scents: vanilla, almond and nutmeg. Canned freestone peaches may be substituted if fresh are not in season. Chill and use directly from the can.
May be prepared in advance.

1 cup sugar
1 cup water
½ teaspoon vanilla extract
4 large, fresh ripe peaches
½ cup heavy cream
¼ teaspoon almond extract

GARNISH:
Freshly grated nutmeg

1. Combine sugar, water and vanilla extract in a skillet large enough to arrange peach halves in one layer. Stir over low heat until sugar dissolves. Bring to a boil and boil 3 minutes.
2. Meanwhile, dip peaches into boiling water to cover for about 30 seconds to loosen the skins. Cool in cold water. Remove skins; cut in half and remove pits. Put into salt water (1 teaspoon to 1 quart) to prevent darkening, then transfer to hot syrup.
3. Simmer peaches in the syrup, covered, for 5 to 7 minutes, or until tender. Remove from heat, cool, then refrigerate in the syrup until ready to serve.
4. Whip the cream with the almond extract until it mounds lightly but is not stiff.

PRESENTATION: Drain chilled peaches and place cavity side up in sherbets or large wineglasses, using 2 peach halves per serving. Top each with a puff of the whipped cream; grate nutmeg lightly over each.

To prepare in advance: Complete steps 1 through 4, up to Presentation. The peaches may be poached a day in advance, but the cream should be whipped no more than 2 hours in advance and chilled.

MENU

Shrimp Tempura

These fried shrimp emerge from a shallow oil bath in a pale and lacy coating. The doily effect results from an unusual procedure in frying. Drops of batter are sprinkled onto the hot fat with the fingertips and the coated shrimp are carefully laid onto it; more batter is sprinkled over the shrimp as they fry. Unusual and absolutely delicious, especially when dipped into sweet-and-sour Tamarindo Sauce. The shrimp are Hawaiian in origin, and the sauce recipe, acquired in Peru, is surprisingly Chinese. The Shrimp Tempura may be prepared in advance if necessary, but are best when fried and served immediately.

May be prepared in advance.

        8 raw jumbo shrimp (about ½ pound)*
           Salt
        1 large egg

* If jumbo shrimp are not available, buy the largest possible and use 3 or 4 in each "doily" for an individual serving. Frying time will be slightly less.

¼ cup unsifted all-purpose flour
¼ cup cornstarch
¼ cup water
⅛ teaspoon salt
   Peanut oil for shallow frying

ACCOMPANIMENT:
Tamarindo Sauce (below)

GARNISH:
4 sprigs of watercress

1. Shell shrimp, leaving tail attached. With a sharp knife split each partway through the back and devein. Open, and, using a slapping motion, flatten shrimp with the broad side of a heavy knife or Chinese cleaver. Score lightly twice in a crisscross pattern to prevent curling when frying. Lay flat on a plate, ready for frying. Sprinkle lightly with salt.

2. Prepare batter by hand, using a wire whisk or fork. Beat egg just enough to blend yolk and white. Stir in flour, cornstarch, water and the ⅛ teaspoon salt, but do not overmix. (A few flour lumps should remain, which is part of the secret of the crisp lacy coating on these shrimp.) Make batter just before using.

3. Using a large skillet, heat only enough peanut oil, so that it is no more than ¾ inch deep, to 380°. Test by dropping a little batter in; if it rises to the surface at once, the oil is ready. (An electric skillet is ideal for easy temperature control.)

4. To fry, dip fingertips or a fork into batter and sprinkle (actually swirl) over oil quickly several times, to cover a 4-inch area. This forms a lacy background. Holding shrimp by the tails, dip 2 at a time in batter so each is lightly coated, then lay carefully on the lacy batter. Sprinkle more batter on the top of the shrimp. Cook for 1 minute; turn and cook 1 minute longer, or until cooked through and batter is crisp. It will remain pale. Drain on paper toweling and keep warm in a 350° oven while frying remainder, 2 shrimp at a time. (If you are skillful, you may be able to handle 2 "doilies" at a time.)

Note: The oil must be very hot and no more than ¾ inch deep, or the batter will disperse instead of clinging together somewhat.

If this happens, pull the droplets of batter together with a fork. If you find this impossible to achieve, eliminate this step; simply dip the shrimp individually into the batter, then fry. You will then have shrimp tempura done the usual Japanese way.

PRESENTATION: Place each double-shrimp "doily" on a salad plate and garnish with a sprig of watercress. Accompany with individual small dishes of Tamarindo Sauce. The shrimp are to be eaten with a fork, each bite dipped into the warm sauce.

To prepare in advance: Complete step 1, up to making the batter. (For perfect results, the batter must be made just before using.) Prepare Tamarindo Sauce. The shrimp may be fried, cooled and then reheated in a 350° oven, but are best when freshly fried.

TAMARINDO SAUCE

    4 tablespoons sugar
2½ teaspoons cornstarch
   ½ teaspoon monosodium glutamate
   1 teaspoon imported soy sauce
   2 tablespoons red wine vinegar
   1 teaspoon catsup
   1 cup water

1. Mix sugar, cornstarch and monosodium glutamate in a small saucepan. Gradually stir in soy sauce, vinegar, catsup and water, in order named.

2. Cook over medium heat, stirring constantly, until mixture thickens and becomes clear, about 3 minutes.

Serve warm. Yield: 1¼ cups.

Note: This sauce keeps well for weeks. Put in a screw-top jar and refrigerate, but heat before using.

Pork Shreds and Bamboo Shoot Soup

This soup takes less then 10 minutes to make. It has an appealing subtle flavor due mainly to the Oriental sesame oil. The watercress is not only a garnish but an integral part of the recipe. *May be prepared in advance.*

¼ pound lean pork (loin is preferred, but any cut will
    do)
2 tablespoons cornstarch
2 cups water
1 small canned bamboo shoot, sliced thin and cut in
    matchlike strips (2 tablespoons)*
1 scallion, chopped (including tender part of the
    green)
1 tablespoon soy sauce (Kikkoman brand preferred)
½ teaspoon red wine vinegar
½ teaspoon monosodium glutamate
½ teaspoon Chinese or Japanese sesame oil†

GARNISH:
Sprigs of watercress (coarse stems removed)

1. Cut the pork across the grain into paper-thin slices (or as thin as you can) and then into ¼-inch strips. (This is easier if meat is partially frozen.) Dredge with cornstarch, shaking off excess.

2. Bring the water to a boil in a 2-quart saucepan. Stir in the bamboo shoot, scallion, soy sauce, vinegar and monosodium glutamate. Return to a boil and add pork strips. Stir immediately to prevent slices from sticking together. Reduce heat and simmer about 5 minutes, or until pork is cooked through.

* Store unused bamboo shoots in water in a screw-top jar in the refrigerator. Will keep several weeks if water is changed every few days.

† Oriental sesame oil is available in Chinese or Japanese grocery stores. The light-colored sesame oil found in health stores is not the same. Don't omit; it is a necessary contributor to the unusual flavor of the soup. It must be stirred in just before serving, as the essence evaporates quickly.

PRESENTATION: Stir sesame oil and a few sprigs
of watercress into the hot soup and serve immediately
in small soup bowls or cups.

To prepare in advance: Complete all steps up to Presentation;
cool and reheat when ready to serve.

Poached Sea Bass

This is sea bass poached to perfection in a Chinese manner and
served in a soy-sauce mixture, pleasantly flavored with fresh
ginger and sesame oil. For poaching, the fish must be absolutely
fresh, or the flesh will turn soft when cooked. Purchase it the
same day you cook it.

May be partially prepared in advance.

    2 fresh sea bass, each weighing 1 ¼ to 1 ½ pounds
    ⅓ cup peanut oil
    4 cloves garlic, crushed with the flat of a knife
       A 1-inch piece of fresh ginger, thinly sliced and cut
          in fine strips*
    2 teaspoons sesame oil*
    3 tablespoons imported soy sauce*
    2 teaspoons sugar
    1 teaspoon monosodium glutamate
       Salt

GARNISH:
    4 scallions, cut in 1 ½ -inch pieces and shredded (use
          part of the green)

   1. Rinse the sea bass, removing any scales. Leave the head and
tail on. Set aside.
   2. Heat the peanut oil in a small skillet over medium heat. Add

* Both Oriental sesame oil and fresh ginger are available in Oriental food
stores. Fresh ginger may also be found in Spanish markets and some supermarkets. Imported soy sauce (from China or Japan) is fermented naturally and is
required. That made in the United States is chemically treated and inferior.

the garlic and sauté until barely golden; remove garlic and discard. Remove oil from heat and cool. Then add the ginger and sesame oil; set aside.

3. Combine soy sauce, sugar and monosodium glutamate in a small bowl; set aside.

4. To poach the fish, use a fish poacher or any pan with a lid, just large enough to accommodate the fish (2 medium skillets will work as well). Put enough water in the pan to cover the fish by at least 1 inch, and bring to a boil. Place the fish on the rack of the fish poacher, if you are using one, or slip directly into the pan. Immediately turn off the heat, cover, and let stand in the water 15 to 20 minutes, or until the fish is cooked through. At this point the fish will flake easily. It should be opaque, but still moist, not dry.

5. Using two spatulas, remove the fish to heated serving platter. Pour the reserved soy-sauce mixture over the fish. Sprinkle lightly with salt. Quickly reheat the ginger and oil until ginger turns golden, and pour it over the fish (it may splatter, so be careful).

> PRESENTATION: Garnish the sea bass with the shredded scallions and serve immediately. To serve, remove heads and cut each fish in two, giving each guest half. Spoon some of the sauce and garnish over each portion.

Note: The Chinese always poach a fish with the head intact to help retain the natural juices. If preferred, remove the head (and discard) before bringing to the table.

To prepare in advance: Complete steps 1 through 3, up to poaching the fish.

Steamed Rice, Chinese Style

The Chinese prefer long-grain rice and cook it without salt, oil or butter. Cooked properly, the rice is somewhat chewy and each grain is separate.

May be prepared in advance.

1 cup long-grain rice* (not converted)
1 cup cold water

1. Measure rice and put into a 2-quart saucepan. Wash, rubbing rice through your fingers, in several changes of water, until the water is almost clear. (This rids the rice of excess starch and prevents scorching when cooking.) Drain off water.

2. Add cold water in amount equal to rice (for this recipe, 1 cup) and level the rice with your hand. Bring to a boil over high heat, then cover and reduce heat to as low as possible. Let the rice steam for 13 to 15 minutes. Do not remove the lid during this period. Rice is done when water is absorbed and rice is dry. (At the minimum time, tip the pan to see if any water is remaining; if so, cook a minute or two longer to evaporate.) Remove pan from heat and let stand, covered, 15 minutes longer to complete the steaming process.

3. After this second steaming period, remove lid and stir with a fork to fluff and separate the grains. Yield: 3 cups.

Note: Rice may be kept hot in a warm oven up to ½ hour.

PRESENTATION: Serve in a heated serving bowl.

To prepare in advance: Complete step 1 a few hours in advance; be certain to drain rice. Or cook and steam rice, turn into a casserole and cool. Reheat, loosely covered, in a 350° oven until heated through. Sprinkle with 2 teaspoons water before placing in the oven to create some steam.

Tossed Watercress

A simple salad, a delicious one. Sherry gives the greens an intriguing flavor.
May be partially prepared in advance.

* Carolina long-grain rice is excellent.

    1 bunch watercress (about 6 ounces)
    2 tablespoons peanut oil
    1 tablespoon dry sherry
    ¼ teaspoon salt (scant)
    ½ teaspoon monosodium glutamate

1. Rinse the watercress, drain and store in refrigerator wrapped in a towel to absorb remaining moisture.
2. Combine peanut oil, sherry, salt and monosodium glutamate; set aside.
3. When ready to serve, cut watercress across in thirds, using both leaves and stems. Put stems in salad bowl. Add reserved dressing and toss lightly; then add the watercress leaves and toss lightly again. (Overtossing will cause the tender leaves to bruise.)

   PRESENTATION: Serve immediately on individual chilled salad plates.

To prepare in advance: Complete steps 1 and 2, up to tossing the greens.

Winter Raspberries with Sour Cream and Curaçao

The limited number of ingredients belies the cool beauty of this dessert. Sour cream from the carton is spooned into small parfait glasses, topped with frozen raspberries, barely thawed, and "spiked" with orange curaçao.
May be prepared in advance.

    1 package (10 ounces) frozen red raspberries in syrup
    ½ pint dairy sour cream
    6 teaspoons curaçao, or other orange-flavored liqueur

1. Divide the sour cream among 4 small parfait glasses, carefully dropping the cream from an iced-tea spoon into the bottom of the glasses (not on the sides). Chill.

2. Thaw the berries according to package directions until barely thawed. Divide among the parfaits and top each with 1½ teaspoons curaçao. (This is a small serving, and parfait glasses may be only half filled.)

PRESENTATION: Serve cold, placing the parfaits on small plates. Include long-handled spoons.

To prepare in advance: Complete all steps in the following manner: Spoon cream into glasses any time during the day and refrigerate. But thaw berries only enough to separate, timing remaining thawing according to package directions (overthawed berries become limp). Spoon into glasses; add curaçao, and refrigerate. By the time you are ready to serve, the berries will have thawed sufficiently.

Menus and Recipes
for Six

MENU

FIRST COURSE: · *Avocado on the Half Shell with Jellied Consommé*

MAIN COURSE: · *Standing Rib Roast, an Unusual Way*
Watercress Garnish
· *Scalloped Oysters*
· *Shredded Carrots Braised in Butter*
· *Purée of Potatoes*

DESSERT: Swedish Apple Shortcake
Coffee

· Quick and Easy Recipe

Avocado on the Half Shell with Jellied Consommé

Simple and expandable. Surprisingly, this appetizer tastes better when made with the highly concentrated canned bouillon than with a rich homemade one. The salty crisp bacon garnish is an important ingredient. Do not omit it.
Must be partially prepared in advance.

3 ripe medium avocados, chilled*
1 can (10½ ounces) beef consommé (undiluted) (Campbell's preferred)

GARNISH:
3 strips bacon, sautéed and crumbled

1. Chill the consommé in the can for several hours (overnight preferred) to jell. Do not dilute. When jellied and ready to use, stir with a fork to make it glisten.

* As avocados generally appear in the market in an unripe stage, purchase several days ahead, and when slightly soft and ready to eat, refrigerate to stop the ripening process.

63

2. Sauté bacon until very crisp; drain on paper toweling. Crumble with your fingers.

3. Cut avocados in half lengthwise. Remove pits but do not peel. Rub cut surface with lemon juice if allowed to stand more than a few minutes before serving.

> PRESENTATION: Place each avocado half on a small plate. Fill cavity with jellied consommé and top with crumbled bacon. You will need teaspoons for the avocado.

To prepare in advance: Complete steps 1 and 2, up to preparing the avocado. Even when rubbed with lemon juice, the avocado may darken if cut too far in advance. If bacon softens, reheat to crisp.

Standing Rib Roast, an Unusual Way

Here is a perfect way to prepare roast beef: crusty brown on the outside, juicy and rare all the way through. The roast is first spread with a highly seasoned paste, then placed in a very hot oven for less than 1 hour. Then the oven is turned to warm and the beef is left for at least 1 hour to complete cooking, but up to three hours longer if more convenient. With this method of roasting there will be no drippings for gravy—a tablespoon or two of concentrated juices, but not enough to be useful. The high temperature and baked-on crust seal the juices inside the roast, where they ought to remain.

Must be prepared in advance.

>   A 6- to 6½-pound first-cut beef roast (short ribs removed before weighing)
> 1 tablespoon dry mustard
> 1 tablespoon salt
> 2 tablespoons bacon drippings (solidified) or soft butter
> 1 clove garlic, put through a press

GARNISH:
Sprigs of watercress (½ bunch)

1. If possible, buy supermarket beef at least 3 or 4 days ahead, as it needs to age for better flavor. To store, wrap loosely in plastic wrap and refrigerate.

2. Remove from refrigerator and allow to stand at room temperature at least 3 hours before roasting. Combine dry mustard, salt, bacon drippings or butter and garlic. Using a knife, spread over beef on all sides, including ends. Place in a roasting pan, fat side up, the ribs forming a natural rack. Let stand until ready to roast.

3. At least 2 hours before serving, preheat oven to 400° and place beef in lower third of oven. Roast 40 minutes, then, without opening oven, turn heat down to 200° and let remain undisturbed for at least 1 hour, but 2 or 3 hours longer if desired.

PRESENTATION: To serve, remove roast from oven, place on a heated serving platter and garnish as desired with sprigs of watercress. Serve immediately, carved in thin (or thick) slices, giving each person a portion of the crusty outside slices and a little of the watercress.

Note: There is no need to let the beef stand to "collect" itself, as the long period of waiting has already provided this.

Scalloped Oysters

An excellent accompaniment for roast beef, these are simply fresh oysters heated briefly with buttery, crumbled saltines, oyster liquor, parsley flakes and a whiff of nutmeg. The secret to the goodness is browning the butter to a hazelnut color and keeping the saltines in fairly large pieces.

May be partially prepared in advance.

¼ pound butter
2 cups crumbled saltine crackers (broken the size of oyster crackers)
1 pint fresh oysters (any size, but small preferred), drained but liquor reserved
½ teaspoon salt
⅛ teaspoon pepper
Freshly grated nutmeg (a sprinkling)
2 tablespoons chopped parsley
1 tablespoon milk

1. Melt butter in a heavy 2-quart saucepan over low heat; then shake the pan until the moisture has cooked away and the butter begins to turn brown. Remove from heat. Add crumbled crackers and stir until coated well.

2. Using a shallow buttered casserole (3- to 4-cup size), spread half of the buttered crackers on the bottom, then the oysters, sprinkling them with salt, pepper, nutmeg and half the parsley. Spread remaining crackers on top and top with remaining parsley.

3. To bake, combine milk and ¼ cup oyster liquor; pour over the top and place in the upper third of a preheated 375° oven for 10 to 15 minutes or until the oyster edges curl and saltine pieces are crisp again.

PRESENTATION: Serve hot directly from the casserole.

To prepare in advance: Complete steps 1 and 2, up to baking. Add the milk and oyster liquor just before you put into the oven. (If added earlier, the liquid would soften the crackers, and they should remain somewhat crisp.)

Note: For this menu (if you do not have 2 ovens) when ready to serve, leave roast in and turn oven to 375°; remove in 10 minutes and add the oyster casserole. This will ensure that the beef stays hot while the oysters are baking.

Shredded Carrots Braised in Butter

These are delicious. The carrot juices and butter unite as a sauce, making the shredded carrots taste as if they had been born in butter.
May be prepared in advance.

    1¼ pounds carrots (about 10 long slim ones)
      8 tablespoons sweet butter (¼ pound)
      ½ teaspoon sugar (less if young and sweet)
         Salt to taste

1. Scrape carrots with a vegetable peeler, then shred on the medium blade of a grater. Cook immediately to keep from discoloring unless you use a stainless peeler and grater. (If you do they will retain their color for hours.)
2. Melt butter in a medium-size heavy skillet. Add shredded carrots and sauté over medium heat, stirring to coat at first. Sprinkle with sugar. Salt to taste. Cover and cook 2 to 3 minutes; then turn off heat and let stand, covered, 5 minutes to steam. They should be tender-crisp.

PRESENTATION: Turn into a heated serving dish. The bright orange carrots need no garnish.

To prepare in advance: Complete steps 1 and 2, but steam only 3 minutes and remove lid after steaming; stir to cool quickly. When ready to serve, reheat quickly. They are best, however, when the cooking process is not interrupted.

Purée of Potatoes

These potatoes are intentionally very soft and creamy—puréed, not mashed—and extra rich with butter.
May be prepared in advance.

2¼ cups packaged potato flakes (about)*
2½ cups water
  8 tablespoons sweet butter (¼ pound)
  1 teaspoon salt
  1 cup milk (at room temperature)

1. Bring water, butter and salt to a boil in a 2-quart saucepan. Remove from heat and add milk.

2. Add the potato flakes and when liquid is absorbed, stir lightly with a fork. Do not whip. The potatoes should mound like lightly whipped cream. If too soft, add a few more flakes. Yield: 4 cups.

> PRESENTATION: Turn into a warm serving dish and serve immediately, or hold in a warm oven up to ½ hour. If preferred, leave potatoes in the saucepan, cover and set back on turned-off burner. Will keep warm at least 20 minutes.

Swedish Apple Shortcake

The "shortcake" here is similar to shortbread cookies in texture and flavor. The crust is filled with apple slices from a can and dusted with cinnamon, then baked until bubbly. The dessert is served while it still has a blush of warmth, or what the Swedes call "new cold." It is topped with unsweetened and unflavored whipped cream, which amazingly cuts the richness of the pastry.
May be prepared in advance.

  1 cup butter, softened (½ pound)
  ⅓ cup confectioners' sugar
  ¾ cup cornstarch
  ¾ cup unsifted all-purpose flour

* French's Country Style Mashed Potatoes were used to test this recipe. The amounts of ingredients added are different from those on the package.

2½ cups canned sliced cooking apples, drained*
⅔ cup sugar
½ teaspoon ground cinnamon
½ tablespoon butter, cut in small chunks

GARNISH:
Lightly whipped cream, unflavored and unsweetened (½ pint)

1. To make the pastry, cream the 1 cup butter until very soft. Sift together the confectioners' sugar, cornstarch and flour. Work into butter with a pastry blender or with fingers to form a soft dough. Press into a 9-inch Pyrex pie plate (first refrigerate about 15 minutes if too soft to work with). Press edges flat with a fork. Do not flute as the dough is very rich and any high edges will burn. Chill at least 1 hour.

2. Remove pastry shell from refrigerator and fill with drained sliced apples. Mix the sugar and cinnamon together and sprinkle over the top. Dot with the remaining ½ tablespoon butter.

3. Bake in the middle of a preheated 350° oven for 50 to 60 minutes, or until the apples are bubbling and the crust is lightly browned. Remove from the oven and place on a rack to cool in a warm place.

PRESENTATION: Serve just as the shortcake has cooled (about 1 hour after removing from oven). Cut in wedges and top each serving with unflavored and un-sweetened whipped cream.

Note: You will not be able to cut this dessert in perfect wedges as the crust crumbles easily. However, the dessert will look attractive when the whipped cream is spooned over the top. For this reason the dessert should be cut and assembled in the kitchen.

To prepare in advance: Complete step 1 (the pastry) any time, even the day before. Or complete steps 1 through 3, up to Presentation, and reheat until barely warm in a 200° oven. Bake as close to serving time as possible, however, as the shortcake is best when freshly made.

* I use Comstock brand sliced apples, not their apple-pie filling.

MENU

Peruvian Squash Soup

There are tiny flecks of hot red pepper in this pale yellow soup. Its merits: inexpensive, unusual, delicious, easy. I learned it from my cook in Peru, who made it often for herself for lunch. *May be prepared in advance.*

> 1 pound yellow summer squash, either straight or
>   crookneck (small size preferred)
> 2½ cups water
> 1½ teaspoons salt (scant)
> 1 small onion, finely chopped (⅓ cup)
> 1 tablespoon butter
> ½ to 1 teaspoon minced, fresh hot red peppers*
> ¼ cup Crème Fraîche (see Index II) or evapo-
>   rated milk†
> 1 tablespoon milk

* If fresh hot red peppers are not available, use canned. These vary in strength so start with ¼ teaspoon and add to taste.

† In Peru, 5 tablespoons evaporated milk are used instead of the Crème Fraîche and milk, but I find the above a fresher-tasting version.

ACCOMPANIMENT:
Tiny salted crackers (purchased)

1. Remove ends from squash and discard. Wash squash, but do not peel or seed. Cut in ½-inch chunks.
2. Cook squash, covered, in the 2½ cups water with the salt added, until very tender, about 10 to 15 minutes. Cool slightly, then pour into blender container with liquid and purée on low. It should not be too fine. Return to saucepan.
3. In a small skillet, slowly sauté the onion in the butter until edges are lightly browned. Add minced peppers and sauté a few seconds longer. Add to squash along with Crème Fraîche and milk. Let stand until ready to serve, then heat until very hot but not boiling. Taste and add additional salt if necessary. Yield: About 1 quart.

PRESENTATION: Ladle the hot soup into small soup bowls. Pass a bowl of tiny salted crackers.

To prepare in advance: Complete steps 1 through part of 3, up to heating and serving. The soup may be prepared days in advance and kept refrigerated in a 1-quart screw-top jar.

Zarzuela de Mariscos, a Catalan Shellfish Dish

Catalonia is a region in Spain in which Barcelona is located. It has a long coastline along the Mediterranean and is noted for its seafood cookery. Zarzuela, one of the best known dishes, contains a variety of seafood simmered in a savory sauce. This version, although made mainly with shellfish (lobster, shrimp and mussels), also contains pieces of cod and rings of squid. The advance preparation of the seafood (which is eased if the fish store does most of it), and *sofrito* (sauce), takes longer than the actual cooking, which is about 15 minutes.
May be partially prepared in advance.

2 live lobsters (each 1 ¼ to 1 ½ pounds)
½ pound raw shrimp (or at least 12)
1 pound squid
½ cup olive oil
2 large onions, minced (1 ½ cups)
4 cloves garlic, put through a press
4 medium tomatoes, skinned, seeded and finely chopped (1 ½ cups) (see Index II)
¼ cup finely chopped parsley
1 teaspoon salt
½ teaspoon ground white pepper
⅛ teaspoon ground saffron
2 cups dry white wine
24 mussels, cleaned (see Index II)
1 pound cod, halibut, haddock or any firm white fish, boned and cut the size of sea scallops (cod preferred)
2 tablespoons brandy or rum (or to taste)

ACCOMPANIMENT:
Toasted Garlic Bread (recipe on page 74)

1. To prepare the lobsters, cut each in two lengthwise, leaving shell on, then across into serving pieces (3 to 4 per half). Twist off claws and cut in 3 sections at joints; crack each section and loosen meat. Remove intestinal vein and sac near head, but leave the greenish-brown tomalley (liver) and the black coral (roe) if there is any. To save time, have the fish store do whatever of the above is possible.

2. Shell and devein the shrimp, leaving tail intact.

3. Purchase the squid already cleaned. If this is not possible, proceed as follows: Gently pull head and tentacles from the bodies of the squid. Cut the eyes from the tentacles and pull out insides from the body, along with the spine bone and ink sac; discard. Remove the mottled purple skin under running water. Cut the body in ½-inch rings and leave the tentacles joined in one piece.

4. Heat the olive oil in a large flameproof casserole or Dutch

oven. (A large Chinese wok if you have one is perfect.) Add the onion, garlic, tomatoes and parsley. Sauté slowly, stirring frequently until onions and tomatoes have reduced to a rich-looking sauce (the *sofrito*), about 30 minutes. Season with the salt, pepper and saffron.

5. Turn heat to high. Add the lobster, flesh side down, and the squid; sauté a minute or two to absorb some of the oil. Stir in the wine. Cover tightly; reduce heat and simmer 10 minutes.

6. Add the shrimp, mussels and fish; turn heat high until the mixture boils, then cover, reduce heat and simmer 5 minutes, or until the mussels are opened and the shrimp are cooked through. Discard any unopened mussels. Taste and correct seasoning. Stir in the brandy or rum to taste. (May be held 15 minutes in a 200° oven.)

> PRESENTATION: Serve directly from flameproof casserole (if using one), or transfer to a heated serving dish. Ladle into deep plates or soup bowls, previously heated. Pass Toasted Garlic Bread to soak up the succulent juices.

To prepare in advance: Complete steps 1 through 4, up to cooking the seafood.

Hearts of Romaine in Lemon Juice

The idea here is Turkish—a refreshing accompaniment for the Zarzuela. Prepared in the following manner, upright in a bowl, the romaine provides an attractive edible decoration for the table as well. This unusual salad is often served as a first course in Turkish restaurants, where it is referred to as "French lettuce." *May be prepared in advance.*

> 2 or 3 heads of romaine lettuce
> ¼ cup lemon juice (juice of 2 lemons)
> 4 teaspoons water, or dilute to strength desired
> 1 teaspoon salt

1. Remove coarse outer leaves of romaine and save for another salad. Separate the remaining inner leaves from the stalk and wash in a sink filled with water. Drain briefly in a colander. Then roll the leaves up in one layer in a terry-cloth towel, turning ends of towel under. Refrigerate in the towel to absorb any remaining moisture. Store at least 1 hour to crisp.

2. To make the dressing, add water to the lemon juice to dilute to the strength desired, and salt. Divide and pour into two small bowls (glass is most attractive) that are deeper than they are wide so that they accommodate the romaine standing upright (stem ends down).

Note: Depending on the size of the bowls, you may need to increase the amount of dressing.

PRESENTATION: Arrange the chilled leaves upright in the two bowls, reforming the heads as well as possible (the smaller leaves in the center). Place each on a plate and put at either end of the dining table. The leaves are to be plucked one by one by the guests and eaten out of hand. Tipping the leaf will allow some of the lemon juice to run down the stem to the wider end.

To prepare in advance: Complete all steps, up to Presentation. If desired, the bowls of romaine may be put on the table before serving the first course.

Toasted Garlic Bread

Hot, robust and crusty, this Italian bread is toasted in the broiler, but is not entirely a last-minute problem. Raw cloves of garlic are rubbed directly into the bread for full garlic flavor.
May be prepared in advance.

1 long loaf (10 ounces) Italian bread, 4 to 5 inches in
   diameter
Garlic cloves, peeled
Softened butter

1. Cut the bread diagonally in 2½-inch-thick slices, then cut
each slice in half.
2. Place under preheated broiler (in lowest position) until one
side is lightly toasted; turn and toast other sides. Remove. Watch
carefully, as slices burn easily. Toasting may take less than 1 minute on each side.
3. Cut off tip of a clove of garlic and rub over the toasted surface of the bread so that part of the clove is grated off into the
bread. Do this sparingly, but on all cut sides.
4. Spread softened butter on cut surfaces. Store in a plastic
bag until ready to reheat. Then reheat in the oven (any temperature) until hot.

PRESENTATION: Place in a napkin-lined basket
and serve immediately.

Note: If preferred, when toasting second side, do not brown.
Just let slices dry out slightly and get rough. Rub with garlic and
spread with butter. Then to reheat, place under broiler to brown
and heat at the same time. (This is the preferred method as there
is less chance for the bread to dry out; it should be soft inside,
crisp outside.)

Sangría

Sangría is a refreshing chilled red wine drink. It is a very
popular Spanish beverage, second perhaps only to *jerez* (sherry),
which originated in Spain. This recipe makes 2 quarts. On a hot
summer evening you may need more.
Must be partially prepared in advance.

½ lemon, cut in thin half-slices
½ orange, cut in thin half-slices
½ large apple, cored and cut in thin wedges
2 ounces brandy (¼ cup)
½ ounce curaçao or other orange-flavored liqueur (1 tablespoon)
⅓ cup sugar (superfine is best)
1 bottle dry red wine (Spanish preferred but any will do), chilled
1 quart club soda, chilled

1. Combine fruits, brandy, curaçao and sugar in a pitcher early in the day. Let stand at room temperature to marinate until nearly ready to serve, then refrigerate to chill pitcher.
2. When ready to serve, stir in chilled wine, then soda and fill pitcher with ice cubes. Yield: 2 quarts.

PRESENTATION: Pour into water goblets or wine bells, spooning a little of the fruit into each.

To prepare in advance: Complete step 1, up to adding the wine and soda.

Note: This makes a refreshing light drink; if a stronger wine flavor is desired, reduce the amount of club soda by 8 ounces.

Soufflé Caramel with Crème Fraîche

This impressive dessert is Spanish in spirit only—the caramel makes it so—but the recipe is English, a variation of the French classic *Île Flottante*, or floating island. It is a lovely fluff of soft meringue baked in a caramel-lined mold, which when inverted becomes liquid burnt sugar. A bowl of Crème Fraîche, that matured thick French cream, is passed to double the agony of riches.
Must be prepared in advance.

Caramel Syrup (recipe below)
6 egg whites, at room temperature (¾ cup)
A few drops lemon juice
¾ cup sugar (superfine preferred)
1 teaspoon vanilla extract

ACCOMPANIMENT:
Crème Fraîche (recipe below)

1. Make Caramel Syrup and prepare soufflé dish as indicated in that recipe.
2. Beat the egg whites until foamy; then beat in lemon juice and continue to beat until they stand in soft peaks. Add the sugar, a tablespoon at a time, beating well after each addition. Continue beating until mixture is stiff and glossy, and the sugar is dissolved. Beat in the vanilla.
3. Spoon about a fourth of the meringue into the soufflé dish lined with Caramel Syrup and spread with the back of the spoon to form a smooth lining. Add remaining meringue. It should fill the soufflé dish to the top; level off any excess with a spatula.
4. Place the soufflé dish in a pan of hot water. Bake in the lower third of a preheated 275° oven for 30 to 35 minutes, or until set and top is lightly browned. Remove and let cool on a rack at room temperature, then refrigerate at least 3 to 4 hours, but no longer than 12.

Note: As the meringue bakes it will rise above the mold, but will settle as it cools.

5. When ready to serve, loosen edges of meringue with the tip of a wet knife, then unmold on a deep plate. The caramel will have turned to syrup and will trickle down the sides of the meringue, forming a pool in the serving dish.

PRESENTATION: Bring to the table and cut in wedges with a wet cake server. Spoon some of the Caramel Syrup over each serving and pass a bowl of Crème Fraîche to provide a second sauce.

CARAMEL SYRUP

½ cup sugar
2 tablespoons plus 2 teaspoons water
¼ teaspoon cream of tartar

1. Combine sugar, water and cream of tartar in a small heavy saucepan. Cook over medium heat, without stirring, until the sugar is melted and turns amber. (Do not allow it to become too dark or it will be bitter.) Remove from heat.
2. Have ready a warmed 1½-quart soufflé dish and pour the hot syrup into it. Rotate it so that the bottom and sides are completely covered with the syrup. Set aside upside down to harden.

Crème Fraîche

Crème Fraîche is a French cream richer than our whipping cream in butterfat, with a somewhat mature and nutty flavor. (The English have a similar thick cream which they refer to as double cream.) It is so thick you can stand a spoon in it. It is often served "as is," or with a little sugar added, to be ladled over fresh berries for a simple but perfect dessert. But it has other uses, too. It can be boiled without curdling (unlike our commercial sour cream) and can be kept for weeks without turning (unlike our whipping cream). Here is an approximation of the lovely French cream.
Must be prepared in advance.

1 pint heavy cream
2 tablespoons buttermilk (not the "butterflake" variety)

1. Pour the cream into a screw-top jar. Add buttermilk. Stir to blend. Cover loosely and let stand at room temperature until it has thickened. (On a hot day this might take as little as 8

hours, or in a cool place it could take as long as 24. Count on its taking about 12 hours.)

Note: If you must hurry it along, put jar in unlighted oven for an hour or so, then let stand at room temperature. Do not put over pilot light of range, as the cream may taste "cooked."

2. When thickened, stir, cover tightly and store in the refrigerator at least 12 hours before using. This cream may be kept refrigerated up to 1 month. It may even thicken more; undoubtedly it improves with age. Yield: 1 pint.

MENU

FIRST COURSE: *Hot Mixed Antipasto*
Pencil-Slim Bread Sticks

MAIN COURSE: • *Hot and Spicy Shrimp Sauté*
• *Fresh Green Beans with Lemon Butter*
• *Potatoes in Cream au Gratin*
Crusty French or Italian Bread

DESSERT: • *Fresh Blueberries with Lemon Sherbet*
Espresso with Lemon Twist and a Few Drops Anisette

• Quick and Easy Recipe

Hot Mixed Antipasto

Most Italian antipasti are composed of cold ingredients; this one is baked, and it is served after it has cooled only slightly. It is a combination of typical Italian ingredients: sliced tomatoes, anchovies, artichoke hearts, black olives and stuffed mushrooms, all arranged decoratively in a shallow casserole, then bathed in olive oil and sprinkled with fresh bread crumbs before baking.
May be partially prepared in advance.

3 large tomatoes
6 canned anchovy fillets, drained
Salt
Freshly ground pepper
½ teaspoon oregano
1 package (9 ounces) frozen artichoke hearts, cooked (method below)
Juice of ½ lemon (1 tablespoon)

12 black Italian olives (any variety)
Stuffed Mushrooms (recipe below)
 1 cup fresh bread crumbs (see Index II)
 3 tablespoons olive oil

ACCOMPANIMENT:
Pencil-slim bread sticks (purchased)

1. Cut thin slices from the ends of the tomatoes and cut each center part into two slices (about 1 inch thick). Discard ends. Arrange in a circle, not overlapping, in a large, shallow greased casserole. Sprinkle lightly with salt and freshly ground pepper and the oregano. Place an anchovy over each tomato, pointing toward the center.

2. Fill center of casserole with the cooked artichokes. Sprinkle them with the lemon juice and salt lightly.

3. Arrange the black olives around the artichokes. Place the stuffed mushrooms between the tomatoes at the outer edge of the casserole.

4. When ready to bake, sprinkle bread crumbs over entire casserole and dribble the olive oil over the bread crumbs. Bake in the upper third of a preheated 375° oven for 15 to 20 minutes, or until the crumbs are lightly browned. Let stand a few minutes. It should not be piping hot. In fact, this appetizer is very good cooled to room temperature.

PRESENTATION: Serve directly from the casserole, giving guests a sampling of each food. Put bread sticks in a tall glass and pass.

To prepare in advance: Complete steps 1 through 3, up to sprinkling with crumbs and baking. (If crumbs are added too far in advance, they will absorb the moisture from the vegetables.)

Stuffed Mushrooms

> 6 large fresh mushrooms (about 6 ounces)
> 3 tablespoons olive oil
> 6 green olives (no pimiento), finely chopped
> 2 anchovy fillets, finely chopped
> 2 tablespoons fine dry bread crumbs

1. Rinse mushrooms quickly, but do not peel. Remove stems and scoop out a little of the inside of the cap to make room for the filling. Reserve stems and trimmings.
2. Heat the 3 tablespoons olive oil in a small skillet; add mushroom caps and toss just long enough to coat. Remove and reserve oil.
3. Finely chop the reserved mushroom stems and trimmings. Sauté in the reserved oil over medium-high heat until they exude their juices, about 5 minutes. Then stir in chopped olives, chopped anchovies and bread crumbs. Spoon into mushroom caps. Cool.

Cooked Frozen Artichoke Hearts

Remove the artichokes from the carton; run under cold water to separate. Then drop, frozen, into 2 quarts unsalted boiling water. Return to a boil and cook rapidly for 5 minutes, or until tender. Drain in a colander, and run cold water over to cool rapidly.

Hot and Spicy Shrimp Sauté

Two sauces: one a marinade, properly garlicky; the other a fine combination of condiments. A favorite of mine.
May be partially prepared in advance.

2½ pounds large raw shrimp
¼ cup olive oil
4 cloves garlic
1 teaspoon salt
3 tablespoons lemon juice
1 tablespoon Worcestershire sauce
¾ teaspoon Tabasco sauce
8 tablespoons butter (¼ pound)

GARNISH:
Chopped parsley

ACCOMPANIMENT:
French or Italian bread, heated or not

1. Shell and devein shrimp, leaving last segment and tail on.

2. To make a marinade, put the garlic cloves through a press into the olive oil. Add salt; stir. Add shrimp, turn to coat, then marinate the shrimp in this mixture, refrigerated, for at least 2 hours, but 12 hours in advance if preferred.

3. Combine the lemon juice, Worcestershire sauce and Tabasco sauce in a small bowl; set aside.

4. To sauté the shrimp, melt the butter in a 10-inch heavy skillet; drain marinade from shrimp into the butter. Heat over high heat until the foam from the butter subsides (do not let the butter brown). Add the shrimp, sauté quickly until shrimp are pink and tails curled up, about 5 minutes, stirring several times to cook evenly. Remove the shrimp to a heated serving platter, leaving juices in the pan.

5. Stir reserved lemon-juice mixture into the pan juices, and stir about 1 minute, scraping up browned bits from bottom of skillet. Immediately pour over the shrimp.

PRESENTATION: Sprinkle chopped parsley over shrimp. Spoon the juices over the shrimp as they are served. Crusty French or Italian bread is a must to accompany the shrimp—serve heated if desired. Either way, put bread in oven a few minutes to crisp the crust.

To prepare in advance: Complete steps 1 through 3, up to sautéing the shrimp.

Fresh Green Beans with Lemon Butter

The beans are prepared first by a special blanch-and-refresh method of boiling and cooling, which preserves their bright-green color and natural taste. Best of all, this process can be done well in advance. All that is left to do is reheat the beans in butter at serving time. Here they are made piquant with a generous squeezing of lemon juice.

May be partially prepared in advance.

  1½ pounds fresh green beans, blanched and refreshed
        (method below)
   5 tablespoons butter
   2 tablespoons lemon juice (1 lemon)
      Salt to taste

1. Put blanched and refreshed beans in a skillet over medium-high heat; toss carefully to evaporate any moisture that still clings.
2. Stir in butter and continue to heat, tossing until beans are hot. Do not brown. Remove from heat and sprinkle with lemon juice; salt to taste. Continue tossing to distribute evenly.

Alternate heating method:
1. Dry beans on paper toweling.
2. Melt butter over very low heat. Add beans; gently fold over and over to distribute, then heat very slowly, uncovered, until hot, about 10 to 15 minutes. Sprinkle with lemon juice and salt; toss to distribute.

PRESENTATION: Serve immediately in a heated serving dish, arranging beans lengthwise as best you can.

To prepare in advance: Blanch and refresh beans. Leave at room temperature on paper toweling if using the same day; or store in plastic bags with crumpled paper toweling to absorb excess moisture.

Blanching and Refreshing Fresh Green Vegetables

This French technique is used to ensure fresh flavor, proper texture and bright green color; it permits cooking the vegetable well in advance, with only finishing touches left for the last minute.

Blanching: Drop prepared vegetables into a pot of boiling salted water, adding salt when water comes to a boil. For 1½ to 2 pounds of vegetables you will need 6 quarts of water and 3 tablespoons coarse salt. Larger quantities of vegetables should be done in 2 or 3 batches—or water and salt increased proportionately, if you have a pot larger than 8 quarts.

The success of this technique depends on the great quantity of water. The faster the water returns to a boil after the vegetables are added, the greener and fresher tasting they will be. Boil uncovered, rapidly, but not vigorously. It is also a good idea, before blanching, to run the prepared vegetables under hot water from the faucet to take off the chill and warm slightly.

Refreshing: Immediately plunge the cooked vegetable into an equal quantity of cold water. This will stop the cooking immediately, set the color and preserve the texture and flavor.

After a few minutes, remove, drain off the water and dry on a towel. Store at room temperature (preferably) until ready to use, or if done the day before, store in the refrigerator in a plastic bag with crumpled paper toweling to absorb the extra moisture. The vegetables will retain reasonable freshness up to 48 hours, but they are best when precooked the same day and left at room temperature.

Asparagus, Green Beans, Broccoli and Peas

Trim, cut and otherwise prepare vegetables for blanching and refreshing according to directions below. Boil, using the length of time indicated as a guide. Taste frequently after the minimum time and continue to cook until just tender. Then refresh.

ASPARAGUS: 6 TO 10 MINUTES

Cut off the dry end of the butt, which is fibrous, about 1 inch. Using a small sharp knife, peel off the skin and tough outer flesh, especially toward the butt end (you will need to go nearly ⅛-inch into the stalk here). This method makes the entire stalk edible, not just the tips (taste a raw piece to be certain you have trimmed enough).

Note: For very thin stalks this method is easier: Place an asparagus stalk on a cutting board to the left of the sink. Holding tip with left hand, run a vegetable peeler down the length of the stalk. Shake off peel into sink. Rotate slightly and repeat procedure. A bowl of water is helpful to rinse off peels that cling to the peeler blade.

Arrange the spears evenly in bundles 3 inches in diameter, according to thickness. Tie with string at both ends. When blanching, add bundles containing thicker stalks first, then those containing the thinner ones. When cooked, spears should bend a little, but not be limp. Remove the bundles with tongs rather than pouring off with water, as the tender tips break easily.

Skillet method: Use a large skillet and add loose spears, arranged in one direction. When cooked, carefully pour off water and add an equal amount of cold water to refresh. (This technique is suitable only for small quantities—less than 1 pound—depending on capacity of skillet.)

GREEN BEANS: 6 TO 8 MINUTES

Cut tips off both ends and leave whole. (An easy way is to line up 5 or 6 at a time on a cutting board and cut off tips from one end; turn beans, line up and trim off other ends.) When cooked, the beans should be tender but retain the slightest suggestion of crispness. (Winter beans will take 8 minutes.)

BROCCOLI: 5 TO 6 MINUTES

Soak in salt water (1 teaspoon to 1 quart) for 30 minutes to remove any insects and dislodge soil. Trim off tough end of the stalks and discard the coarse leaves (or cook later as greens). Cut off the stalks 1½ to 2 inches below the florets and peel the stems (thickly if necessary) to expose the tender pale-green flesh. Taste a raw piece; if fibrous, you have not peeled deep enough. Cut each stalk in half, then lengthwise in halves or quarters. Divide the florets in quarters if large, and peel off any tough skins with a paring knife. They will come away easily. The thinly cut stalks will cook in the same length of time as the tender florets. When cooked, both should be slightly crunchy. Be gentle when refreshing, as the florets may mash with careless handling.

PEAS: 4 TO 8 MINUTES

Remove peas from pods just before cooking as they lose quality rapidly. When cooked they should be tender. (The great variation in time depends on size and age of peas.)

Potatoes in Cream au Gratin

This is a delicious and attractive way of serving potatoes, and one of the easiest to prepare. Baked potatoes are scooped out into a shallow casserole, seasoned with onion and moistened with heavy cream, then covered with Swiss cheese and crumbs for a golden top.

May be partially prepared in advance.

    4 large Idaho baking potatoes (2 pounds)
    6 tablespoons butter, softened
    ½ small onion
  1 ½ teaspoons salt
      White pepper to taste
    ½ cup heavy cream
    ½ cup grated Swiss cheese (2 ounces)
  1 ½ tablespoons Buttered Bread Crumbs (method below)

1. Bake the potatoes in a preheated 400° oven for 50 minutes to 1 hour, or until soft. Cut in half lengthwise to let steam escape and let cool just enough to handle.

2. Scoop out each potato with a spoon into a 1 ½-quart shallow ovenproof casserole that has been spread with 4 tablespoons of the softened butter. Potatoes should be coarse, not mashed.

3. Grate the onion directly into the potatoes, using a medium grater. Add the salt; add pepper to taste. Mix lightly to distribute. Cool, uncovered.

4. When ready to serve, dot with 2 more tablespoons of the butter and dribble the heavy cream over the top. Sprinkle with cheese, then with buttered crumbs.

5. Bake in the upper third of a preheated 375° oven for 15 to 20 minutes, or until lightly brown and piping hot.

PRESENTATION: Serve hot from the casserole. The cheese and bread crumbs give it a golden top and no additional adornment is necessary.

To prepare in advance: Complete steps 1 through 3, up to preparing for baking. This can even be done the day before if desired. Store in the refrigerator loosely covered. (If covered tightly, the potatoes may taste "old.") Bring to room temperature before baking.

BUTTERED BREAD CRUMBS

Melt ½ tablespoon butter in a small skillet; stir in 1½ tablespoons fine dry bread crumbs. Stir over low heat until golden.

Fresh Blueberries with Lemon Sherbet

Couldn't be simpler or more refreshing. Fresh lemon is squeezed over store-bought sherbet to heighten the lemon flavor. *May be partially prepared in advance.*

    1 pint fresh blueberries
    1 pint lemon sherbet
       Juice of 1 lemon (2 tablespoons)

    ACCOMPANIMENT:
    Thin crisp cookies (a good store-bought variety)

1. Pick over blueberries; discard any stems. Rinse, drain in a colander and refrigerate.
2. When ready to serve, spoon sherbet into a chilled serving bowl. Sprinkle the lemon juice over the top by cutting the lemon in half and squeezing through the end of a clean towel to strain the pulp and seeds (or squeeze and put through fine strainer). Pour blueberries on top.

   PRESENTATION: Serve immediately at the table in individual sherbets. Or, if preferred, assemble in the individual dishes.

To prepare in advance: Complete step 1. Or complete steps 1 and part of 2, up to adding the blueberries. Put bowl in freezer, covered with plastic wrap.

MENU

FIRST COURSE: · *Jellied Consommé, Cream and Caviar*
Black Bread
Butter

MAIN COURSE: *Oriental Pressed Duck*
· *Scallion Flowers*
Fried Rice, New Delhi Style
Lettuce Hearts with Tarragon Cream

DESSERT: · *Brandied Black Cherries*
French Vanilla Ice Cream
Coffee

· Quick and Easy Recipe

Jellied Consommé, Cream and Caviar

This combination of flavors is remarkable: the tell-all is in the title. The recipe is expandable and may be adapted for any size dinner party. I have even served it at cocktail parties on a large platter set in crushed ice to keep the consommé from melting.
Must be partially prepared in advance.

1½ cans beef consommé (10½-ounce size) (undiluted)
1½ cups Crème Fraîche (see Index II)
3 ounces black caviar (any quality)

GARNISH:
Thin slices of lemon peel

ACCOMPANIMENT:
Any good black bread and butter

1. Chill consommé in the can several hours (overnight preferred) to jell.

2. Make Crème Fraîche at least one day in advance.

3. Stir consommé with a fork to break up, then spoon onto *chilled* salad plates (especially attractive on ones with a wide, flat edge). Spread to cover center area. Spoon Crème Fraîche in center of consommé, dividing evenly among the plates. Top the cream with a spoonful of caviar.

> PRESENTATION: Garnish the caviar with a thin slice of lemon peel and serve immediately. You will need teaspoons to eat this. Accompany the appetizer with any good black bread, slices halved or quartered, and butter.

To prepare in advance: Complete steps 1, 2 and part of 3, up to adding the caviar (it may run if added too far in advance). Chill individual plates until ready to serve. The plates must be chilled before filling or the consommé will melt.

Note: When desiring to use this recipe for fewer or more guests than 6, keep these proportions in mind: For every 2 persons you need ½ can consommé, ½ cup Crème Fraîche and 1 ounce caviar plus 2 slices lemon peel for garnish.

Oriental Pressed Duck

Within this recipe is a method for boning a cooked duckling which, surprisingly, is easy to do. The boned duck is "pressed," then fried and coated with a sauce containing soy sauce, almond extract and sherry, and covered thickly with chopped toasted almonds. At one *chifa* (Chinese restaurant) in Lima, Peru, duckling is served similarly with a coating of thickened soy sauce which has been flavored with the Chinese spice star anise. In a South Seas restaurant in Denver, toasted sesame seeds replace the almonds. Many combinations are possible.

Must be partially prepared in advance.

A 5-pound Long Island duckling
Water (about 4 quarts)
A 2-inch slice of fresh ginger (optional)
Tops of 6 to 8 scallions used in garnish
2 tablespoons dry sherry
1 tablespoon salt
Flour
3 tablespoons peanut oil
Almond Sauce (recipe page 93)
½ cup Toasted Chopped Almonds (2½ ounces) (method below)

GARNISH:
Scallion Flowers (page 94)

1. Rinse the duckling and pull out excess fat from the cavity. Prick lightly with a fork at ½-inch intervals to allow fat to escape while duck simmers. Split down back to open, using a heavy knife or poultry shears. Remove wing tips.

2. In a large kettle, add enough water to cover the duckling; bring to a boil and add the ginger (if used), scallion tops, sherry and salt. Carefully submerge the duckling and return to a boil, then reduce to simmer and cook, covered, for 30 minutes. Remove from heat and let stand in the stock at least 1 hour. Remove; reserve ½ cup stock.

3. To bone the duckling, lay breast side down on a platter. Using a small sharp knife, start working away the flesh from both sides of the backbone and remove the rib cage. Pull or cut away the cartilage in the breast and massage out any stray bones in this area. Pull out the leg and thigh bones, and cut off the tough skin at the bottom of the legs. The wings are the most difficult. Don't worry; just pull out the bones as best you can and press the loose pieces of meat along the sides to form as uniformly an even piece as possible. Cut off fatty part of neck, and fold remainder up over meat.

Note: This is easier than it sounds. It is similar to removing the meat from a boiled chicken, but here you are leaving the skin on and trying to keep the meat in one large piece.

4. Place a piece of waxed paper on top of the meat, then a baking sheet and put a heavy weight on it to "press" the duck. (Several heavy cans of tomatoes work well.) Let stand until cold, then remove weights and refrigerate.

5. When duckling is chilled (or next day if desired), cut in half and dust both sides with flour. Heat a large skillet until very hot; add half the oil and half the duckling, skin side down. Sauté over medium-high heat until browned and skin is crisp. Then turn over and brown other side. Remove to an ovenproof platter, skin side up, and repeat process with other half, using the remaining oil. Keep warm.

6. Spoon the hot Almond Sauce over the duckling and spread evenly to cover. Sprinkle with the Toasted Chopped Almonds.

PRESENTATION: Serve hot (best) to lukewarm. Cut duckling in 2-inch squares to serve. Garnish platter with Scallion Flowers.

To prepare in advance: Complete steps 1 through 4, up to sautéing; or, if desired, sauté the duckling and leave at room temperature until ready to serve. Then reheat in a 375° oven for about 10 minutes, or until hot. Add sauce and almonds just before serving to keep the skin crisp.

ALMOND SAUCE

    2 tablespoons imported soy sauce*
    1 tablespoon cornstarch
    ½ cup duck stock (reserved)
    ¼ cup dry sherry
    ½ teaspoon almond extract

Mix soy sauce and cornstarch in a small saucepan. Gradually stir in reserved, cooled duck stock. Cook and stir over

---

* Imported soy sauce from China or Japan is fermented naturally and is necessary here. That made in the United States is treated chemically and is inferior. Kikkoman is a good Japanese brand available in most supermarkets.

medium heat until thickened, about 3 minutes. Remove from heat. Stir in sherry and almond extract. Use while hot.

Note: Sauce may be prepared in advance and reheated. Add sherry and almond extract after reheating.

TOASTED CHOPPED ALMONDS

Place any amount of whole blanched almonds in one layer in a dry, heavy skillet. Stir over low heat until light brown. Remove from heat and cool. Do not overbrown, as they continue to darken as they cool. Chop coarsely and store in a covered jar in the refrigerator or freezer.

SCALLION FLOWERS

6 to 8 scallions

1. Wash and remove any dry skin on scallions. Cut off ½ inch above roots and use green tops for simmering duck as for Pressed Duck, leaving about 4 inches for the "flower."
2. Cross-slit both ends about 1 inch deep. Soak in ice water 1 hour. Ends will open like a flower. Drain.

Fried Rice, New Delhi Style

This is an unusually good version of fried rice. To prevent a blending of flavors, each ingredient is stir-fried separately, then combined, enabling it to retain its own identity. The result is a dish of great subtlety that is typical of Chinese cuisine at its finest. You will note the addition of hot peppers, and the absence of a characteristic ingredient, soy sauce. The recipe is authentic Chinese as typically prepared in restaurants in New Delhi, India.
May be prepared in advance.

4 cups cold steamed rice, Chinese style (1¼ cups un-
     cooked) (see Index II)
   Peanut oil
¼ pound lean pork, cut in ¼-inch cubes (½ cup)
   Salt
¼ pound shelled and deveined raw shrimp, coarsely
     chopped (½ cup)
1 teaspoon dry sherry
4 scallions, chopped (including tender part of green)
2 small green chilies, seeded and chopped, or 1 table-
     spoon canned green chilies
2 large eggs
¼ teaspoon monosodium glutamate
1 teaspoon sugar

1. Prepare rice at least 6 hours ahead and store in refrigerator
until ready to use. It must be cold.

2. Heat a small skillet (6½ to 7 inches) and when very hot
add 1 teaspoon peanut oil. (If you add the oil before pan is hot,
the meat may stick.) Add the pork, sprinkle with ¼ teaspoon
salt and stir and fry until cooked through, about 5 minutes. Remove pork, drain and put to one side on a large plate.

3. Rinse the skillet; wipe dry with a paper towel. Heat skillet
and when almost smoking add 2 teaspoons oil; stir in shrimp,
sprinkle with ¼ teaspoon salt and stir and fry 2 to 3 minutes, or
until cooked through; drain and place beside pork on the plate.
Sprinkle the shrimp with the sherry. Rinse skillet and dry.

Note: If, before chopping, shrimp has a strong odor, let stand
for 10 minutes in water to cover with a pinch of soda added.

4. Using 1½ teaspoons oil, stir-fry scallions and chilies in the
same manner as above, and remove when still tender-crisp, in
about 1 minute. Set aside on dish with pork and shrimp. (If using
canned chilies, add to plate without frying.) Rinse and dry skillet.

5. Using 1 egg at a time, break into a teacup; add ⅛ teaspoon
salt and beat with a fork just to blend yolk and white. Heat the
same skillet over medium heat; add 1 teaspoon oil and pour in the

egg. Tip skillet to cover the bottom evenly. Turn heat to low. When set, but still moist on top, remove from heat. (It must not brown.) Turn out onto a plate, cut in ¼-inch strips, then cut each strip diagonally into ¼-inch strips to shred. Repeat with other egg. Set aside.

6. When ready to fry the rice, heat a large skillet (9 to 10 inches) or a Chinese wok if you have one, until almost smoking; add 2 tablespoons oil. Add the cold rice and stir to break up lumps. Stir rapidly so that the rice will not stick to the pan, adding a little more oil if necessary. Sprinkle with 1 teaspoon salt, the monosodium glutamate and the sugar. Continue stirring so that the rice grains separate, become coated with oil and brown lightly, about 5 minutes.

7. Add reserved pork, shrimp, scallions, chilies and shredded egg. Fold and stir with a fork to distribute evenly and heat through about 3 to 5 minutes longer. (Taste and add additional salt if necessary.)

PRESENTATION: Spoon into a heated serving bowl and serve immediately. Do not cover.

Note: If desired, the fried rice may be kept warm, uncovered, in a 200° oven up to ½ hour before serving.

To prepare in advance: Complete steps 1 through 5, up to frying the rice. Or, complete all steps; turn into an ovenproof casserole; cool. Then cover and refrigerate. Reheat, loosely covered with foil, in a 350° oven about 15 minutes, or until hot. (Sprinkle with 2 teaspoons water before reheating.) The rice is best, however, when fried and served immediately.

Lettuce Hearts with Tarragon Cream

A simple salad: crisp lettuce hearts are the only greens, with an uncomplicated sour cream and mayonnaise dressing.
May be prepared in advance.

Iceberg lettuce, solid heads, broken into bite-size
chunks (enough to make 1 ½ quarts)
½ cup Blender Mayonnaise (recipe below)
¼ cup dairy sour cream
½ teaspoon dried tarragon, crushed
½ teaspoon salt
Dash of Tabasco sauce
1 teaspoon lemon juice

GARNISH:
Chopped parsley

1. Remove core from lettuce; pull off leaves in chunks, using
only the compact inner leaves. Chill in a salad bowl until ready
to serve.

2. Combine mayonnaise, sour cream, tarragon, salt, Tabasco
and lemon juice in a screw-top jar; stir well. Chill in jar in
refrigerator several hours to blend flavors. Dressing will keep
several days.

PRESENTATION: Stir dressing and pour over the
lettuce chunks. Fold over until coated. Serve on individual salad plates with a generous sprinkling of

2 large eggs
2 tablespoons lemon juice (bottled is fine)
2 tablespoons white wine vinegar
1 teaspoon dry mustard
½ teaspoon salt
½ teaspoon monosodium glutamate
1 teaspoon garlic salt
3 dashes cayenne pepper
2 cups oil (peanut or vegetable)

1. Put eggs, lemon juice, vinegar, dry mustard, salt, monosodium glutamate, garlic salt and cayenne pepper in the glass container of a blender. Add ½ cup of the oil; cover and blend on high for 5 seconds.

2. Turn blender on low and gradually pour in the remaining oil, almost drop by drop at first. If you add the oil slowly enough you will be able to add all the oil. If not, you probably won't be able to add it all, and the mayonnaise will be a little heavier than it should be, but will still be excellent. The mayonnaise is ready when it will absorb no more oil.

3. Spoon into a 1-quart screw-top jar, cover and refrigerate until cold. It keeps well, refrigerated, for weeks. Yield: about cups.

Menus and Recipes for Eight

MENU

FIRST COURSE: · *Roquefort Salad*
                     Crusty French Bread
                     Sweet Butter

MAIN COURSE: · *Grilled Butterfly Leg of Lamb*
                 · *Avgolemono Sauce*
                 · *Tomatoes Stuffed with Savory Bread Crumbs*
                     Chelo, an Iranian Rice Dish with Currants and
                     Pine Nuts

DESSERT: *Crêpes Lucien*
                 · *Fresh Preserved Lingonberries*
                     Coffee

                     · Quick and Easy Recipe

Roquefort Salad

In France, salads occasionally are offered as a first course, as this particular one was in a tiny bistro on the Left Bank in Paris. The most abundant lettuce in France is a variety similar to our Boston lettuce. The leaves of Boston are tender and velvety, and are delicious served with this Roquefort dressing. Only blue-veined cheese from Roquefort, France, by government regulation, can bear the Roquefort label.

May be partially prepared in advance.

     2 heads of Boston (also called butter) lettuce, to
         make 4 quarts torn greens
     3 ounces Roquefort cheese, crumbled
     1 teaspoon salt
     ¼ teaspoon freshly ground pepper
     ¼ teaspoon dry mustard

3½ tablespoons red wine vinegar
⅔ cup peanut oil

ACCOMPANIMENT:
Crusty French bread and sweet butter

1. Pull whole leaves from core of lettuce, tearing off and discarding any brown edges. Wash carefully under the faucet to remove the dirt; let drain about 5 minutes in a colander. Shake off excess water. Wrap loosely in paper toweling and store in the refrigerator to crisp. (Since these leaves are delicate, tear them just before tossing.)

2. To make the salad dressing, combine the crumbled Roquefort, salt, pepper and dry mustard in a screw-top jar. Gradually beat in the vinegar with a fork to blend the other ingredients, then add the peanut oil; cover and shake. Set aside at least an hour to meld the flavors.

3. When ready to serve, tear the lettuce into rather large pieces, leaving most of the small leaves whole. They must be dry. Put into the salad bowl. Shake the dressing to blend, then pour it over the lettuce. Toss gently with a salad fork and spoon, long enough to coat the leaves, but not to bruise or wilt them.

PRESENTATION: Serve immediately in shallow soup bowls (for easier eating) or on individual salad plates. Pass sliced French bread and sweet butter. Heat to crisp the crust, but serve at room temperature.

To prepare in advance: Complete steps 1 and 2, up to tossing the salad. This tender lettuce is best washed, chilled and used the same day. The dressing should be made only a few hours before using.

Grilled Butterfly Leg of Lamb

This is boneless lamb cut to lie flat, marinated overnight (or longer), then broiled and served with a delicate Greek lemon sauce called *avgolemono*. The boneless lamb is easily carved in thin slices and arranged overlapping on a heated platter. In summer grill over charcoal if preferred.

Must be partially prepared in advance.

An 8-pound leg of lamb, boned and "butterflied"
¼ cup red wine vinegar
½ cup olive, peanut or vegetable oil
6 cloves garlic, put through a garlic press
1 tablespoon salt
10 peppercorns, coarsely crushed

GARNISH:
Sprigs of parsley

ACCOMPANIMENT:
Avgolemono Sauce (recipe below)

1. Have the butcher bone and "butterfly" the lamb (split so that the meat lies flat in one large piece). He should also peel off the parchmentlike covering called the fell, and trim away all but ¼ inch of fat beneath it. The meat will vary in thickness, but after it is broiled and carved, it will make a handsome platter.

2. Combine the vinegar, oil, garlic, salt and pepper in a non-metal pan large enough to accommodate the meat spread flat. Put the lamb in the marinade, turn over once, cover with plastic wrap, then with aluminum foil, and marinate in the refrigerator at least 24 hours before cooking, turning occasionally.

3. Remove from the refrigerator and let lamb come to room temperature before broiling.

4. Preheat broiler 15 to 20 minutes, with broiler rack in place, about 4 inches below the source of heat. Then remove lamb from marinade, drain and place on hot broiler rack, fat side down. Broil 15 minutes; turn and broil 15 to 20 minutes longer for medium-rare lamb. Test with a knife in the thickest part, and if not done sufficiently, broil a few minutes longer. The lamb should be charred in places; however, watch carefully so it does not catch on fire.

PRESENTATION: Remove lamb to a carving board, and carve across the grain into ¼-inch-thick slices with a knife held on a slant. The uneven thickness of the meat itself will provide both medium-rare and well-done slices. Arrange overlapping on a hot serving platter, garnished with sprigs of parsley. Spoon a little warm Avgolemono Sauce over each serving and and pass the remainder.

To prepare in advance: Complete steps 1 through 3, up to broiling, or broil and keep warm in a low oven, then carve. The meat may be held in the marinade up to 48 hours.

AVGOLEMONO SAUCE

May be prepared in advance.

> 1 tablespoon cornstarch
> Juice of 1 lemon (2 tablespoons)
> 5 egg yolks (unbeaten)
> 1 teaspoon salt
> ⅛ teaspoon cayenne pepper
> 1 teaspoon dried mint leaves, crushed
> 2 cups chicken broth (canned if preferred)

1. In a 1-quart heavy saucepan, dissolve the cornstarch in the lemon juice (cut lemon in half and squeeze through a clean towel to strain the pulp and seeds, or squeeze and strain through a fine strainer if preferred). Add egg yolks, salt, cayenne pepper and dried mint leaves. Stir with a wire whisk to blend, then stir in chicken broth.

2. Stirring constantly, cook over medium heat until the mixture begins to thicken and coats a spoon (it should not approach a boil). Remove from heat, and use immediately, or set over hot, but not boiling, water to keep warm until ready to serve. Yield: about 2½ cups.

P R E S E N T A T I O N :   Pour into a warm sauceboat, to
be spooned over the lamb.

To prepare in advance: Complete all steps. Cool, cover and
refrigerate. When ready to serve, reheat slowly until warm (do
not let boil).

Tomatoes Stuffed with Savory Bread Crumbs

When a commercial baker supplies excellent seasoned bread
stuffing, why prepare your own? Fresh tomatoes are hollowed,
stuffed with the seasoned and buttered crumbs, then baked
briefly. Good and easy.
May be partially prepared in advance.

    8 medium tomatoes, ripe but firm (2½ pounds total)
       Salt
    2 cups commercial bread stuffing mix (Pepperidge
       Farm brand preferred)
    9 tablespoons butter (¼ pound plus 1 tablespoon)

1. Slice off the top quarter from the stem end of each tomato
which includes the hard core; discard or save for salads. Gently
run an index finger around the inside of each to release the juices
and force out the seeds. Salt lightly and turn upside down on a
rack to drain. Let stand at least 1 hour.
2. Melt butter in a medium skillet. Add the bread stuffing and
sauté over medium heat, stirring constantly with a fork, until the
crumbs are lightly toasted.
3. Fill the tomatoes with the crumb mixture. Arrange in an
oiled, shallow baking dish (a 10-inch pie plate will hold eight).
4. Bake in the upper third of a preheated 375° oven for about
15 to 20 minutes, or until tomatoes are barely cooked. The tomato
skins should appear wrinkled.

Note: For this menu, if a broiler-oven combination is used, set
tomatoes in oven while the lamb is being broiled. The intense heat

will cook the tomatoes in a shorter time, 5 to 8 minutes. (Watch carefully so crumbs do not overbrown.)

> PRESENTATION: Serve hot, without garnish, directly from the baking dish. Overhandling may make them split.

To prepare in advance: Complete steps 1 and 2 any time, but do not fill tomatoes more than an hour or so before baking, as the crumbs should remain crisp.

Chelo, an Iranian Rice Dish with Currants and Pine Nuts

Countries where rice is a staple often produce interesting variations in preparing it. Iran is no exception, and *chelo* (the Persian word for "steamed rice") is a case in point. Here rice is cooked in a way that produces a golden, crisp crust in the bottom of the pan, while the top remains fluffy and white. This crust is considered the choice part and each guest must be served some of it. For this menu, the rice is steamed with the addition of currants and garnished with toasted pine nuts. It is, however, special without these additions.

May be prepared in advance.

2 cups long-grain rice (Carolina type)
3 tablespoons salt
8 tablespoons butter (1 stick)
1 teaspoon oil
2 tablespoons yogurt
¼ cup currants

GARNISH:
Toasted Pine Nuts (recipe below)

1. Measure rice and put in a 4-quart heavy saucepan. Wash rice, rubbing it through your fingers in several changes of water until the water is almost clear. (This rids the rice of excess starch

and prevents the crust from sticking to the pan when cooking.) Cover with water by at least 1 inch and add 2 tablespoons of the salt; stir. Let stand at least 2 hours. Turn into a colander and drain off water.

2. Using the same saucepan, bring 2 quarts of water to a boil over high heat. Add the remaining tablespoon of salt, then sprinkle in the soaked rice, keeping the water at a boil. Stir once to keep from sticking to the bottom, then boil over medium heat, uncovered, for 10 minutes. Remove rice from heat and drain in a colander.

3. Melt 3 tablespoons of the butter in the same (dry) saucepan. Stir in the oil and yogurt. Spoon half the rice in lightly, then sprinkle on the currants, and top with the remaining rice. Dot with remaining 5 tablespoons butter, cut in small pieces. Put a double thickness of paper toweling on top of the pan, then a tight-fitting lid. Turn heat to medium and cook until you hear the rice sizzling, 5 to 8 minutes, to form the crust. Then turn heat to as low as possible, and let rice steam 1 hour. (A little shorter or longer time will not matter.)

4. Remove rice and set pan in cold water a few minutes. This will help loosen the crust which has formed on the bottom. Loosen edges around rice with a spatula. Put a serving platter over the top; invert rice onto platter. If cooked properly, the rice should unmold with the crust on top. (If not, no problem— just scrape out the crust as best you can and place on top of rice. It will still be attractive.) Yield: 6 cups.

PRESENTATION: Sprinkle the top with the Toasted Pine Nuts. Mix in when serving. And be certain to give each guest a little of the crisp crust.

To prepare in advance: Complete all steps, but be certain to unmold immediately on an ovenproof platter. Reheat, loosely covered with foil, in a 350° oven for 10 to 15 minutes. (Sprinkle with 1 tablespoon water before reheating to keep rice from being too dry.)

TOASTED PINE NUTS

Sauté 2 ounces of pine nuts in 1 tablespoon butter over medium heat, stirring until lightly browned. Drain on paper toweling. It is not necessary to keep them hot.

Crêpes Lucien

The directions here for making crêpes make them sound more difficult than they really are. This recipe almost takes longer to write about than to follow, and it works every time. Made one by one, the crêpes do take patience, but they may be prepared days ahead and even frozen. Here the delicate crêpes are served cold, wrapped around a filling of cream cheese lightened with whipped cream and lemon juice. They are arranged on a platter and topped with syrupy lingonberries, those wild, tart miniature berries (similar to cranberries) that come from Sweden. An outstanding dessert.

Must be prepared in advance.

> ½ pound cream cheese, softened at room temperature
>   Juice of ½ lemon (1 tablespoon)
> ½ cup heavy cream
> 8 crêpes, at room temperature (recipe below)
>
> GARNISH:
> Fresh Preserved Lingonberries (recipe below)
> Confectioners' sugar

1. Whip the softened cream cheese with a wire whisk to lighten; add the lemon juice (cut lemon in half and squeeze through the end of a clean towel to strain the pulp and seeds). Whip cream until it is stiff, but not buttery; fold into cream cheese mixture.

2. To fill crêpes, put a generous spoonful (about 3 tablespoons) of the cream cheese filling down the center of one crêpe; fold one side over and tuck under filling, then continue to roll up. Place seam side down on a narrow serving platter. Continue fill-

ing crêpes and line up on the platter in one long row, as you complete each crêpe. Cover with plastic wrap and refrigerate until ready to serve.

PRESENTATION: Remove crêpes from refrigerator. Dust generously with confectioners' sugar put through a sieve. Spoon a little of the Fresh Preserved Lingonberries (at room temperature) over the crêpes just down the center. If canned lingonberries are substituted and are not juicy enough, stir in a little water. Put the remainder of the berries in a sauceboat to be spooned over the crêpes as served. (You will need only about half the berries.) Serve on dessert plates with forks.

To prepare in advance: Make crêpes and cook lingonberries. Complete steps 1 and 2, up to Presentation.

CRÊPES

        2 medium eggs
        6 tablespoons unsifted all-purpose flour
      ¼ cup milk
      ¼ cup water
      ⅛ teaspoon salt
        1 tablespoon brandy
        1 tablespoon melted butter
           Butter for cooking the crêpes (about 2 tablespoons)

1. Beat the eggs until light. Beat in the flour, then the milk, water, salt, brandy and melted butter. Strain to remove any flour lumps. Or use a blender if preferred; add ingredients in order given, then blend on low until smooth. Cover and refrigerate at least 2 hours, but overnight if preferred.

2. Using a 6½-inch heavy skillet, heat over medium-high heat until very hot. (It is ready when a drop or two of water skids across the pan.) Then quickly lift the pan off the heat and add about ½ teaspoon butter; rotate pan to cover evenly. Place skillet back on the heat and pour 2 tablespoons of the batter in; quickly

tilt and rotate skillet to cover the bottom evenly. Ideally the batter should barely coat the bottom of the pan, even to letting some holes remain.

Note: If the pan is too hot the batter will sputter and pop; if not hot enough the pancakes will look gummy. The perfect crêpe should be a delicate brown, tender, thin and lacy. If the first is too thick, thin the batter with a little water.

3. Bake over medium-high heat for about 18 to 20 seconds, or until a faint rim of brown shows around the edges. Lift the edge with a small spatula and with the fingers flip over and bake another 10 seconds. (This second side will be a spotty brown.) Tilt pan and turn out, spotty side up, onto a sheet of aluminum foil large enough to wrap all the crêpes.

4. Repeat procedure, buttering the pan before baking each crêpe. Stack on foil evenly as they are baked; cool, then wrap and refrigerate until ready to use, up to 1 week; or freeze a month or so. Either way, they must be brought to room temperature before separating to avoid tearing.

Yield: 10 to 12 crêpes.

Note: A standard coffee measure holds 2 tablespoons liquid and is perfect for measuring the correct amount of batter. A heavy iron skillet makes an ideal crêpe pan. If a slightly different size skillet is used, the amount of batter used per crêpe should be altered, and the number of crêpes will vary accordingly.

FRESH PRESERVED LINGONBERRIES

2 cups fresh lingonberries*
1 cup sugar

* Lingonberries are tiny wild berries from the forests of Sweden; they resemble our cranberry but have a pronounced "woodsy" flavor. The fresh ones will seldom be found outside communities with a large Scandinavian population. They are worth seeking out. The berries are shipped from Sweden packed only in cold water (without preservatives). They keep for many weeks, due to their high acidity. Felix, the largest Scandinavian canner, produces one close to home-preserved; however, it does contain pectin, a thickener. You will need half a 12-ounce jar, if substituted for the fresh. Use directly from the jar. Homemade cranberry sauce also makes an acceptable substitute.

1. Remove any stems from lingonberries and discard any very soft bruised ones. Drain briefly in a colander.

2. Cook the berries in a large saucepan with only the water that adheres after draining. Add the sugar and stir over very low heat until dissolved. Then cook slowly until the berries are soft, about 15 to 20 minutes. Cool. Cover and refrigerate, but bring to room temperature before using.

Note: You will need only about half this amount of the preserved lingonberries for the crêpes. Store remainder in covered jar in the refrigerator (keeps for months). Use over hot breakfast pancakes or as a relish like cranberry sauce.

MENU

FIRST COURSE:	*Ham Mousse Ardennes* *Hot Toast*
MAIN COURSE:	• *Chicken Cutlets with Mushrooms Gruyère* *Fresh Asparagus with Anchovy Butter* *Potato Croquettes*
DESSERT:	*Belgian Plum Tart* *Crème Fraîche* *Espresso*

• Quick and Easy Recipe

Ham Mousse Ardennes

An appetizer with real character: a molded mousse of fragrant, cured, dried raw ham rests under a layer of clear beef aspic. The cold mousse is spooned out of a casserole and spread on fingers of hot toast. The idea is Belgian, from a restaurant in the Ardennes forest.

Must be prepared in advance.

½ envelope unflavored gelatin (1½ teaspoons)
½ cup plus 2 tablespoons chicken broth
½ pound cured, dried raw ham, coarsely chopped (1 cup firmly packed)*
2 tablespoons port wine
1 egg white, whipped until stiff

* Hams of this type are produced in many countries, the most familiar perhaps being the Italian prosciutto. But there are famous hams from the Ardennes in Belgium, the Bayonne from France; there are the *jamón serrano* of Spain and Westphalian ham from Germany. These hams are cured and dried, rather than smoked, and are intended to be served raw. Specialty meat markets or gourmet outlets with a delicatessen sell these, cut in paper-thin slices.

½ cup heavy cream, lightly whipped
1 can (10½ ounces) beef consommé (undiluted)

ACCOMPANIMENT:
Fingers of crustless thick hot toast*

1. Soften gelatin in 2 tablespoons of the chicken broth. Heat remaining broth (½ cup) to nearly boiling, then stir in softened gelatin to dissolve. Let cool 10 minutes.
2. Pour broth into the glass container of an electric blender. Add the chopped ham and 1 tablespoon of the wine; blend until ham is puréed and mixture is smooth. Pour into a mixing bowl.
3. Fold stiffly beaten egg white into the whipped cream; then fold into ham mixture. Pour the mixture into a 1 to 1½-quart serving dish at least 7 inches in diameter; shake slightly to level, then refrigerate until firm.
4. Stir the remaining 1 tablespoon port into the undiluted beef consommé. Carefully dribble the mixture over the molded mousse, so it remains on top. Cover serving dish with plastic wrap and chill until consommé is firm (this will take several hours).

PRESENTATION: Bring the ham mousse in its serving dish to the table. Spoon out portions for guests. Accompany with hot toast, crusts removed and slices cut in thirds. The mousse is to be spread on the bread, so include butter knives.

Chicken Cutlets with Mushrooms Gruyère

Delicate and delicious. Boneless strips of breast of chicken (the "supremes") are ever so lightly sautéed in clarified butter, then baked with white mushroom slices and grated Gruyère. Wedges of lemon are to be squeezed over the chicken before eating to give the dish a subtle fresh lemon flavor. The recipe becomes a Quick and Easy one if the boning is done by the butcher.
May be partially prepared in advance.

* Pepperidge Farm brand Toasting White Bread is perfect.

4 whole chicken breasts (4 pounds) or 2 pounds boneless chicken cutlets
4 eggs beaten with 2 teaspoons salt until frothy
1 cup unsifted all-purpose flour (about)
½ pound butter, clarified (see Index II)
2 cans (4-ounce size) mushroom slices, drained
½ pound Swiss cheese, coarsely grated (2 cups) (do-
 mestic is fine)
1 cup rich chicken broth

GARNISH:
2 lemons, cut in quarters
Sprigs of watercress

1. Bone and remove skin from chicken breasts; pull out the white tendons and cut each breast lengthwise into 6 strips.

2. Immerse chicken strips in the eggs beaten with the salt. Remove one by one, letting excess drip off; then roll lightly in flour.

3. Heat a little clarified butter in a large skillet, and sauté a few strips of chicken at a time over medium-low heat, just until crusty but not colored. Turn with tongs and repeat on other side. (Takes only a minute or two on each side. The secret in the delicacy of this dish lies in not overcooking the chicken.) Arrange one layer deep in 1 or 2 lightly buttered shallow casseroles. Repeat with remaining chicken strips, adding butter as required. Leave drippings in skillet when chicken is removed.

4. Scatter mushroom slices over the chicken and top with the grated cheese.

5. Add chicken broth to butter and drippings remaining in skillet and cook over high heat a minute or two to reduce slightly, scraping up the browned bits at the same time.

6. Pour reduced broth into casserole, but not over chicken. Bake in the middle of a preheated 300° oven until piping hot and cheese is melted, about 15 minutes. Do not overbake.

PRESENTATION: Serve hot from the casserole, garnished with watercress and lemon quarters, the latter to be squeezed over the chicken cutlets at the table. As each portion is served, pour a spoonful of the pan juices over the top.

To prepare in advance: Complete steps 1 through 5, up to adding the reduced broth and baking the casserole.

Fresh Asparagus with Anchovy Butter

Asparagus is delicious, especially when freshly picked. But store-bought asparagus, if handled in the manner described here, will have the same spring flavor. First it must be peeled (the real secret), then precooked according to the blanch-and-refresh method, which permits the asparagus to be cooked in advance, then reheated when you are ready to serve. The butter sauce is an outstanding one made with anchovies and garlic.

May be partially prepared in advance.

> 2 pounds fresh asparagus, any size (but larger takes less trimming), blanched and refreshed (see Index II)
> ½ cup butter (1 stick), clarified (see Index II)
> 3 cloves garlic, peeled and crushed
> 2 large anchovies, finely minced

1. Blanch and refresh asparagus.
2. Clarify butter.
3. Place clarified butter in a large skillet over low heat. Add garlic cloves and cook gently until lightly browned on the edges. Remove and discard garlic. Remove from heat and add anchovies, stirring until partially dissolved.
4. Add asparagus spears, all running in the same direction, roll over in the butter, return to heat and reheat slowly until piping hot.

PRESENTATION: Carefully turn out onto a warm serving platter and pour anchovy butter over the top. Serve immediately.

To prepare in advance: Complete steps 1 through 3, up to heating the asparagus. Cool the anchovy butter and reheat slowly when ready to use.

Potato Croquettes

A bit tedious, but well worth the effort. Potato purée is enriched with egg yolks and butter and scented with garlic, then made into finger logs, crumbed and deep-fat fried. The croquettes may be completely prepared in advance and reheated, but the best ones are fried just before serving.

May be prepared in advance.

Puréed Potatoes (recipe below)
4 egg yolks
6 tablespoons butter, softened
3 teaspoons salt
2 cloves garlic, peeled and pulverized with the salt
½ teaspoon white pepper or a few drops Tabasco sauce
¼ teaspoon freshly grated nutmeg
2 eggs
2 teaspoons oil
½ teaspoon salt
Fine dry bread crumbs
Oil for deep frying

1. Add the egg yolks and softened butter to the cooled potato purée, mixing well with a fork. Do not use a beater as the mixture should not be too creamy. Add the salt-and-garlic mixture, pepper and nutmeg; mix well.

2. Shape into balls about 1½ inches in diameter, then roll on an unfloured board into logs about 1 inch thick. Set aside. (You will have about 40.)

3. Beat the 2 whole eggs, the 2 teaspoons oil and the ½ teaspoon salt together until well blended (or use blender on low).

4. Dip potato logs into the egg mixture to coat; then roll in the dry bread crumbs. Make certain the crumbs are patted on well or

they will float off into the oil when the croquettes are fried. Place, slightly separated, on a baking sheet and let dry at least 1 hour. (This also helps keep the coating on.)

5. To fry, heat at least 3 inches of oil in deep-fat fryer to 400°. Fry the croquettes, a few at a time, until golden. Drain on paper toweling. Then keep warm in a 200° oven while frying remainder.

PRESENTATION:　Place in a heated serving bowl; serve hot.

To prepare in advance: Complete steps 1 through 4, up to frying, and refrigerate, loosely covered, overnight. Or, fry a few hours in advance, then reheat in a hot oven set at any temperature. With this menu, at 300°.

PURÉED POTATOES

3 pounds baking potatoes (7 to 9 medium size)

1. Peel potatoes, cut in quarters. (As you peel them drop into cold water to prevent discoloring.)
2. Drop into boiling salted water to cover and boil until tender, about 20 minutes. When done, they can be pierced easily with a fork.
3. Drain and put through a sieve or potato ricer—this way they will come out fluffy. Return the hot purée to the saucepan. Place over low heat and stir until all the moisture evaporates and the potatoes are really dry. At this point the purée will begin to film over the bottom of the pan.
4. Let cool, uncovered. Yield: 6 cups.

Belgian Plum Tart

An open-faced beauty; juicy perfection in a crust. Like most European tarts, this has a glaze brushed on after it is baked to bring the fruit to an appetizing glisten. The tart is served with thick Crème Fraîche. Don't omit; you'll lose half the pleasure. *Must be prepared in advance.*

    1¼ to 1½ pounds purple damson plums,* cut in half
              lengthwise and pitted
     1 tablespoon sugar
    ½ cup red currant jelly
     3 tablespoons cold water
       Unbaked Pastry Shell (recipe below)

GARNISH:
Confectioners' sugar
Crème Fraîche (see Index II)

1. Arrange plums snugly in circles, cut side up, in a pastry-lined 10-inch quiche pan. Sprinkle with the sugar.

2. Bake in the lower third of a preheated 400° oven for 35 to 40 minutes or until the pastry is lightly browned and plums are tender. Remove and slip off the rim of the pan before cooling on a rack. (To do easily, place tart on a tomato-juice can and slip rim down.)

3. When tart is cool, heat jelly and water in a small saucepan, stirring until the jelly melts; then cook a few minutes until syrupy. Cool slightly and remove any scum. While still warm, brush over the plums. Yield: 1 10-inch tart.

PRESENTATION: Sprinkle the edge of the tart with confectioners' sugar, put through a wire sieve. Cut in wedges to serve. Pass a bowl of Crème Fraîche to be spooned over the tart.

To prepare in advance: The best tarts are the freshest ones, so bake as close to serving time as possible, allowing for the cooling period. However, the pastry may be prepared, put in the pan, then into a plastic bag and refrigerated for a day or two before using. Use chilled.

---

* These are also called prune plums.

Pastry Shell

    1¼ cups sifted all-purpose flour
     2 tablespoons sugar (preferably superfine)
     6 tablespoons butter, softened
     2 tablespoons cold water

1. Combine the flour and sugar in a mixing bowl. Cut in the butter with a pastry blender until it looks like coarse cornmeal. Sprinkle water over mixture, a tablespoon at a time, and stir with a fork until all the flour is moistened and dough comes away from sides and forms a ball. Wrap in waxed paper and chill ½ hour.

2. Roll out on a lightly floured board ⅛ inch thick and a little larger than a 10-inch quiche pan with removable bottom. Line quiche pan with pastry and trim off neatly. Use immediately or return to refrigerator.

MENU

Eggplant Caviar

Russians, I am told, eat this in the summer when fresh caviar is not available. It looks best served in a hollowed-out eggplant, but this is not essential. This particular recipe makes a large quantity, which keeps, refrigerated, up to 2 weeks.
Must be prepared in advance.

  2 large eggplants (1 ½ pounds each)
  ½ cup finely chopped scallions (including tender part
      of green)
  3 tablespoons lemon juice (or to taste)
  2 teaspoons salt
     Dash of white pepper
  1 tablespoon olive oil

GARNISH:
Chopped parsley

SERVING CONTAINER:
1 raw hollowed-out eggplant (method below)

ACCOMPANIMENT:
Black bread (any kind) and whipped butter

1. Prick skins of eggplants twice with a fork. Bake on a baking sheet in a preheated 400° oven until very soft, about 1 hour. Remove from oven and let cool somewhat.

2. When cool enough to handle, cut in half and scoop out the pulp. Mash and beat with a fork until smooth. Discard the skin.

3. Add the chopped scallions, lemon juice, salt, pepper and oil; mix well. Chill overnight. Yield: about 3 ½ cups.

PRESENTATION: Cut a shallow slice lengthwise from the raw eggplant. Run a knife about ½ inch inside the rim, then scoop out the pulp with a spoon. (This is easier than it sounds.) Brush the rim and inside of the shell with lemon juice. Fill with eggplant caviar.

Serve with slices of thickly sliced and quartered black bread, accompanied by a pot of whipped butter and a small bowl of chopped parsley. To eat, spread bread with butter, top with a spoonful of eggplant caviar and sprinkle with parsley.

Smoked Oyster Canapés

I was first served these delicious canapés at ten in the morning with a cup of coffee. Delicious then, but even better at the cock-tail hour.

May be partially prepared in advance.

    2 cans (3 ⅔-ounce size) smoked oysters, drained
   32 small round butter crackers (I use Ritz)
   32 thin slices Cheddar cheese, about 1 inch square

1. Place a drained oyster on each cracker (or two if small). Top with a square of cheese. Arrange on an ungreased baking sheet.

2. Bake in a preheated 400° oven 5 to 8 minutes, just until heated through and cheese is melted. Serve immediately. Yield: 32 canapés.

PRESENTATION: Arrange on a serving tray and pass to guests.

To prepare in advance: Complete step 1, up to baking, at any time; cover with plastic wrap and leave at room temperature.

Beef Stroganoff

This is beef in strips, seared on the outside, rare within, served in a fine rich sauce. There are dozens of recipes for the Russian classic and this one is apparently authentic. The wild rice accompaniment is an American addition, and my preference. The traditional one is fried "shoestring" potatoes. To be at its best, Stroganoff should be made with beef tenderloin, but best-quality sirloin or top round may be substituted.

May be partially prepared in advance.

3 pounds beef tenderloin, sirloin or top round
6 tablespoons butter
2 tablespoons oil
1 pound fresh mushrooms, coarsely chopped
½ cup finely minced scallions (including tender part of green)
8 tablespoons dry white wine (Rhine preferred)
1 pint dairy sour cream, at room temperature
2 teaspoons salt
1½ teaspoons paprika

GARNISH:
Additional sour cream
Chopped scallion tops

ACCOMPANIMENT:
Wild Rice (recipe below)

1. Have butcher trim all fat from beef and cut across the grain in ¼-inch-thick slices. At home, cut into ½-inch strips, and if necessary cut again so strips will be no more than 2 or 3 inches long. Dry on paper toweling.

2. Heat a large skillet over low heat until very hot. Add 3 tablespoons butter and 1 tablespoon oil. Turn heat to medium high, and when foam subsides, add beef a few strips at a time. Do not crowd or the beef will stew in its juices instead of turning brown. Sauté quickly until browned on both sides, about 1 or 2 minutes. Remove and set aside. Sauté remaining beef strips, adding butter and oil as needed. Remove and set aside.

3. Add mushrooms to drippings in skillet (there should be about 3 tablespoons), and sauté over high heat until mushrooms are lightly browned and begin to release their juices, about 3 minutes. Then add the chopped scallions and 6 tablespoons of the wine; cook over high heat a few minutes to reduce liquid to about half, stirring to scrape up the browned juices.

4. Remove from heat and stir in sour cream. Add salt and paprika. Return to heat and heat through gently over low heat but do not boil or the sauce will curdle.

5. When hot add the sautéed beef and juices and reheat again until piping hot—no longer or the meat will be overdone. It should be medium rare. Stir in the remaining 2 tablespoons wine. Taste and correct seasoning.

PRESENTATION: Spoon wild rice at ends of a large, warmed platter. Spoon the Stroganoff in the center. Garnish center with several spoonfuls of sour cream. Sprinkle chopped scallion tops over all. Serve immediately.

To prepare in advance: Complete steps 1 through 3, up to adding the sour cream. Store the mushroom mixture and beef separately, covered, in the refrigerator. Bring to room temperature before adding sour cream and reheating.

Wild Rice

Not a rice at all, but a native grain grown mainly in the Minnesota lake country. Wild rice is difficult to harvest, has a limited production and therefore commands a high price. For this particular menu, it's worth whatever you pay.

May be prepared in advance.

> ½ pound wild rice (about 1½ cups)
> 5 cups cold water
> 2 teaspoons salt
> 4 tablespoons butter

1. Wash the wild rice in cold running water; drain.
2. Put into a 4-quart heavy saucepan; add water to cover, bring to a boil and boil 5 minutes; skim off foam containing hulls; drain.
3. Add the 5 cups cold water and the salt; bring to a boil, uncovered, then reduce heat and simmer 35 minutes, or until the kernels have opened and softened and the rice is tender and flaky. (Overcooking will make the rice mushy.) Drain off any remaining liquid, then stir in the butter and toss until distributed. Yield: about 6 cups.

PRESENTATION: Serve immediately, or, if necessary, return to saucepan. Set, covered, on the turned-off burner. Will keep warm at least 20 minutes.

To prepare in advance: Complete steps 1 through 3, up to Presentation. Cool. When ready to serve, reheat in a colander over boiling water, stirring occasionally with a fork to fluff and heat evenly.

Steamed Peas, the French Way

The lettuce helps preserve the bright green color. The pea pods provide an earthy sweetness.
May be prepared in advance.

       4 pounds fresh peas in the pod
          Several large outside leaves of iceberg lettuce
       8 tablespoons butter (¼ pound)
       1 teaspoon salt
       ½ teaspoon sugar
       1 teaspoon monosodium glutamate

1. To preserve freshness, shell the peas only an hour or two before cooking, saving a few pods to add for flavor. (You will have 4½ to 5 cups peas.)

2. In a large, heavy skillet with a tight-fitting lid, place 2 tablespoons of the butter, cut in chunks. Over this arrange 3 or 4 lettuce leaves, rinsed but not dried. Pour peas and reserved pods on top of lettuce. Add remaining 6 tablespoons butter, cut in chunks, and season with salt, sugar and monosodium gluta-mate. Place lid on top.

3. Turn heat to high and when butter is sizzling and steam has formed, turn heat to low and steam just until tender, about 15 minutes. (The only water necessary is that which clings to the lettuce.) Taste and correct seasoning. These can be held in a 200° oven up to 20 minutes to keep warm.

PRESENTATION: Remove wilted lettuce leaves and pea pods. Serve peas hot with their natural juices.

To prepare in advance: Complete steps 1 and 2, up to steaming the peas. Or, complete all steps and remove lid to cool quickly;

then re-cover so peas will not dry out and wrinkle. Reheat briefly until hot. The best peas are those that are steamed and eaten immediately.

Cucumber Strips on Cucumber Peels

A refreshing salad: crisp cucumber quarters in a simple oil-and-lemon dressing. The cucumbers are served on a bed of peels, a garnish idea I picked up at a Turkish restaurant outside Istanbul. *Must be prepared in advance.*

> 6 small cucumbers
> 1 tablespoon salt
> 6 tablespoons olive oil
> 2 tablespoons lemon juice
>
> GARNISH:
> Cucumber peels
> 8 untrimmed red radishes

1. Peel cucumbers with a vegetable peeler. Reserve the peels.
2. Cut off ends and discard; they are often bitter. Cut each cucumber in quarters lengthwise to make 24 strips total. Place in a bowl and cover with cold water; add the salt, mixing with the fingers to distribute. Place the reserved peels in a separate bowl of cold water. Put a handful or two of ice cubes on top of each bowl and let stand at least 1 hour to crisp, replenishing the ice cubes as they melt.
3. Drain cucumber strips in a colander; drain peels and keep separate. Wipe bowl dry and return cucumbers to it. Add the oil and lemon juice. Again mix with the fingers to avoid bruising, which a utensil might do. Serve immediately, or cover and refrigerate until ready to serve, then mix again.

Note: This is best prepared and served within an hour, as the dressing turns the cucumbers limp if they wait longer. They should be crisp.

PRESENTATION: Drain cucumbers and serve icy cold on a bed of the drained peels on individual salad plates, 3 cucumber strips for each plate. Place a washed red radish (with some of the fresh green tops left on) on each salad plate.

Lemon Vodka

Lemon vodka is available in Russian restaurants in Istanbul. This particular recipe came from an American living in that city. The drink is lemon-scented and pale yellow. Curls of lemon peel and whole black peppercorns give it an inviting appearance. Although the vodka is meant to be drunk straight in small stemless glasses, it is less potent when poured over ice.

Must be prepared in advance.

1 quart vodka
2 tablespoons sugar (superfine is best)
10 whole black peppercorns
Rind of 1 lemon

1. Pour off a shotglass of vodka to make room in the bottle for the remaining ingredients.

2. Add the sugar, peppercorns and lemon peels cut from the lemon in long strips with a lemon stripper.* Or use a small sharp knife to remove the peel, then cut in ¼-inch strips. Replace cap on bottle. Turn bottle upside down several times to dissolve the sugar. Then refrigerate 1 week to 10 days before serving. Keeps for months; however, the peels will lose their color eventually.

PRESENTATION: Bring the chilled vodka in the bottle directly to the table. Pour into small glasses, or over ice. Serve instead of wine with the meal. If preferred, the lemon vodka may be made in a crystal decanter.

* A lemon stripper has a notch in the blade which cuts the rind from a lemon in ¼-inch strips.

Chocolate Mousse in Demitasse

Here is an old and reliable formula for chocolate mousse: 1
ounce of chocolate to 1 egg. It is excellent. The mousse is bitter-
sweet and velvety, almost a solid morsel of chocolate, and portions are necessarily small. Coffee should accompany the mousse.
Must be prepared in advance.

        6 squares (1 ounce each) semisweet chocolate
        6 eggs, separated
        1 teaspoon vanilla extract
           Pinch of salt

1. Melt the chocolate in a small heavy skillet over very low
heat. Remove from heat, stir and set aside to cool slightly.

2. Beat the egg yolks with an electric beater until pale and
thick. (When the beater is lifted, the mixture should fall back in
a ribbon.) Stir in the cooled, melted chocolate and vanilla.

3. Beat the egg whites until foamy; add the salt and beat until
stiff but not dry. Stir about ⅓ the egg whites into the chocolate
mixture to lighten it, then fold in the remainder until no white
traces remain.

4. Spoon into demitasse cups or *pots de crème*. Cover with
plastic wrap or *pots-de-crème* lids. Chill well before serving, at
least 6 hours or overnight if preferred.

> PRESENTATION: Place the cups of mousse on
> their saucers with demitasse spoons on the side. Do not
> garnish, as anything, even whipped cream, interferes
> with the velvety texture.

MENU

FIRST COURSE: *Vegetable Minestrone*
                    Pencil-thin Bread Sticks
                    Butter

MAIN COURSE: • *Crusty Herb-baked Chicken with Artichoke
                    Hearts and Black Olives*
                    • *Orzo, an Italian Pasta*

DESSERT: *Black Walnut Pie*
                    Whipped Cream
                    Espresso

• Quick and Easy Recipe

Vegetable Minestrone

Perhaps a little substantial as a first course, but authentic and appropriate in small servings. The fresh Parmesan cheese garnish is a traditional necessity; slim bread sticks, a pleasant accompaniment. The recipe makes over 2 quarts so you will have a quantity left for another day. Note the special method of preparing the beans which eliminates overnight soaking.

Should be prepared in advance.

   1 cup dried pea beans (about ½ pound)
   2 quarts cold water
     Pinch of soda
   1 can (13¾ ounces) chicken broth
   1 tablespoon salt
   1 teaspoon monosodium glutamate
   ¼ teaspoon freshly ground pepper
   ¼ teaspoon thyme, crushed
   ¼ teaspoon rosemary, crushed
   ½ teaspoon marjoram, crushed

1 medium onion, chopped
2 cloves garlic, finely chopped
2 tablespoons butter
2 cups sliced Pascal celery with leaves, cutting ¼ inch
    thick from leaf end of 1 bunch
¼ cup minced parsley
1 large tomato, chopped
1 cup shredded white cabbage
1 cup *maruzzelle,** cooked *al dente* according to pack-
    age directions

GARNISH:
Freshly grated Parmesan cheese

ACCOMPANIMENT:
Slim bread sticks and butter (purchased)

1. Sort and rinse pea beans. Put into a 4-quart heavy saucepan. Cover with 1 quart of the cold water; add the pinch of soda and bring to a rolling boil; boil hard for 2 minutes. Spoon off the scum. Remove from heat and let stand 1 hour. Do not drain. (This eliminates overnight soaking.)

2. Add remaining quart of cold water, the chicken broth, salt, monosodium glutamate, pepper, thyme, rosemary and marjoram. Bring to a boil, then turn heat down and simmer, uncovered, 1 to 1½ hours or until beans are barely tender. The length of time will depend on the "age" of the beans—the period of time the beans were held in storage before being packaged for selling. Old beans are drier and require longer cooking than recently dried ones.

3. Sauté the onions and garlic in the butter until soft and edges are barely browned. Add to beans, along with the celery, parsley, tomato and cabbage. Stir to mix, then continue simmering 25 to 30 minutes longer, or until celery and cabbage are tender. Skim off any foam. For best flavor, cool and refrigerate overnight before adding the shell macaroni.

---

* *Maruzzelle* is an Italian word meaning "small seashells." Shell-shaped macaroni comes in many sizes. The size recommended here is about ¼ inch in diameter. It is sometimes called *conchigliette*.

4. When ready to serve, add the precooked macaroni. Reheat slowly until piping hot; do not cook further or macaroni will soften. Yield: 2½ quarts.

PRESENTATION: Ladle into shallow soup bowls. Pass a bowl of grated Parmesan cheese to be sprinkled over the top. Serve with crusty, slim bread sticks and butter.

Crusty Herb-baked Chicken with Artichoke Hearts and Black Olives

Here is chicken in disguise; without the bone you wouldn't recognize it because of a delicious and zesty crumb crust, which takes over. You could easily make this with only legs or thighs, or all breasts, but I have always used a whole chicken. The dish is attractively garnished with artichoke hearts and black olives. In fact, there are enough artichokes to consider them a vegetable accompaniment.

May be partially prepared in advance.

>   2 frying chickens, each 2½ to 2¾ pounds, disjointed
>   (method below), plus 4 legs or thighs
> 1½ teaspoons salt
>   1 teaspoon garlic salt
>   ¼ teaspoon freshly ground pepper
> 1½ teaspoons thyme
>   ½ cup grated Parmesan cheese (the bland bottled is
>   best)
>   2 tablespoons minced fresh parsley
>   ½ cup dry bread crumbs from stale French bread
>   whirled in a blender (crusts included)
>   4 tablespoons butter
>   4 tablespoons olive oil
>   ½ cup dry vermouth
>   3 cans (14-ounce size) artichoke hearts
>   16 pitted ripe olives

1. Cut up chickens according to method below. Save the wing tips, back, ribs and neck; add to giblets and freeze to use for stock another day. (The extra legs or thighs are called for to provide 2 pieces each plus seconds for some.)

2. Arrange chicken skin side up in 2 shallow greased casseroles. Pieces should touch but not overlap.

3. Combine salt, garlic salt, pepper and thyme. Sprinkle evenly over the chicken pieces. Sprinkle cheese, parsley and bread crumbs (in that order) over the top. Dot with pieces of the butter and dribble the oil over all. Let stand at least 1 hour for better flavor.

4. Bake uncovered in a preheated 400° oven for 30 minutes. Then dribble the dry vermouth into the casseroles from the side, not on the chicken (¼ cup per casserole). Arrange drained artichoke hearts and olives between pieces. Loosely cover the casseroles with aluminum foil and bake 10 to 15 minutes longer, or until the chicken is tender.

> PRESENTATION: Serve hot, directly from the casseroles, spooning some of the pan juices over the artichokes and chicken as served.

To prepare in advance: Complete steps 1 through 3, up to baking the chicken. Do any time, even the day before. Refrigerate, but bring to room temperature for accurate timing.

To disjoint a chicken: Cut off legs and thighs, then separate at the joint. Cut wings from body at the ball joint so that a strip from the lower breast is attached; remove wing tips. Cut away breast with ribs, then slip the knife between flesh and ribs and remove ribs. Trim away any small bones left attached to the breast. With the knife at the tip of the breastbone, cut down and away to remove the flesh containing the wishbone. Cut breast in half crosswise. This will provide 9 good-sized pieces.

Orzo, an Italian Pasta

Orzo is a barley-shaped pasta. (The word *orzo* actually means "barley" in Italian.) Here it is parboiled in water, then finished off in chicken broth for extra flavor.
May be prepared in advance.

> 2 cups orzo*
> 2 cups boiling chicken broth (canned will do)
>
> GARNISH:
> Chopped parsley

1. Drop orzo into 4 quarts rapidly boiling, salted water. Cook 5 minutes. Drain in a colander, then finish cooking in the boiling chicken broth another 5 minutes, or until pasta is *al dente* (cooked but still slightly chewy). Drain off any remaining broth.

PRESENTATION: Turn into a heated serving bowl and garnish with chopped parsley.

To prepare in advance: Complete all steps; cool. Reheat, covered, in a hot oven until heated through. Stir with a fork to break up.

Black Walnut Pie

Made in the same fashion as pecan pie, this is even better—if that's possible. The recipe for the pastry is good and easy. The amount is generous, so no patching is necessary.
Must be prepared in advance.

* Goodman's Barley Shape egg noodles is a similar product, but Ronzoni brand Orzo has the more traditional shape. Both are U.S. products.

2 eggs, beaten until frothy
1 cup dark corn syrup
1 cup granulated sugar
¼ teaspoon salt (scant)
2 tablespoons butter, melted
1 teaspoon vanilla extract
¾ cup coarsely chopped black walnuts (about 4 ounces)*
Unbaked Pastry Shell (recipe below)

GARNISH:
Unsweetened and unflavored lightly whipped cream (½ pint)

1. Prepare pastry shell.
2. Stir corn syrup, sugar and salt into beaten eggs. Add melted butter, vanilla and chopped black walnuts; mix well. Pour into unbaked pastry shell.
3. Bake in the middle of a preheated 425° oven for 15 minutes. Reduce heat to 350° and bake 30 to 35 minutes longer, or until the tip of a knife inserted near the center comes out clean. (The center will continue to cook and become firm as it cools. If overbaked, the filling will be hard.) Cool on a rack. Yield: 1 9-inch pie.

PRESENTATION: Serve at room temperature. Cut pie in eighths—the servings are small, as the pie is rich. Pass a bowl of lightly whipped cream for garnishing.

UNBAKED PASTRY SHELL

1 cup plus 2 tablespoons sifted all-purpose flour
½ teaspoon salt
6 tablespoons vegetable shortening
3 tablespoons cold water (about)

* Black walnuts have become increasingly scarce, but you will no doubt be able to find them in a gourmet shop, unless you happen to live in the South, where they are more widely available.

1. Combine flour and salt in a mixing bowl. Cut in shortening with a pastry blender until part of it looks like coarse cornmeal (the rest should be the size of small peas). Sprinkle water over the mixture, a tablespoon at a time, and mix lightly with a fork until all the flour is moistened. Stir dough vigorously until it pulls away from the sides of the bowl. Form into a ball.

2. Roll out on a lightly floured board ⅛ inch thick and about 1½ inches larger in diameter than a 9-inch pie plate. Put into pie plate; trim edges to ½-inch overhang, fold under and press edge flat with a fork to make an attractive design.

Menus and Recipes
for Ten

MENU
BUFFET

FIRST COURSE: *Fresh Artichoke Appetizer*
Curry Peas

MAIN COURSE: *Indian Dry Curry*
Sambals
• *Steamed Rice, Indian Style*
• *Tomato and Cucumber Salad, the Turkish Way*
Pappadums

DESSERT: *Fresh Pineapple, Bombay Style*
Black Cherry Garnish
Coffee

• Quick and Easy Recipe

Fresh Artichoke Appetizer

Two large artichokes, and a third for decoration, provide enough nibbles for 10 guests. The artichokes are steamed and cooled, then the leaves are plucked from the core and filled, one by one, with a tasty lemon mayonnaise and garnished with dill. One artichoke is placed in the center of a large platter and the filled leaves are arranged spoke-fashion around it. Easy to do, and perfect finger food for a pre-dinner cocktail hour.

May be prepared in advance.

3 large artichokes
1 teaspoon salt
2 tablespoons lemon juice
1 cup Blender Mayonnaise (see Index II)
  Grated rind of 2 lemons

141

1 teaspoon lemon juice
½ teaspoon garlic salt

GARNISH:
Finely chopped fresh dill or parsley

1. Rinse artichokes in salt water (1 teaspoon to 1 quart of water). Cut off stems at base. Do not trim leaves. Put in saucepan large enough to accommodate all 3 artichokes side by side. Add enough water for steaming, about 1 cup, salt and the 2 tablespoons lemon juice. Bring to a boil, then cover and steam 35 to 45 minutes, or until a leaf can be pulled out easily. Remove and put in cold water to cool immediately, then invert and let drain at least ½ hour.

2. Combine the mayonnaise, grated lemon rind, the 1 teaspoon lemon juice and garlic salt.

3. One by one, pluck leaves from just two of the artichokes and put a dab of the mayonnaise mixture on the base of each leaf. As they are filled, arrange in rows spoke-fashion from the center out on a large platter (overlapping leaf tips). Leave room to place the remaining whole artichoke in the center.

PRESENTATION: Place whole artichoke in center and sprinkle filled leaves with chopped dill weed. (Substitute chopped parsley if necessary, as dried dill weed is not as good as fresh.)

Note: A wooden platter is especially appropriate for this appetizer. Don't discard the whole artichoke after the party. Save and eat the following day, dipping the leaves in melted lemon butter.

To prepare in advance: Complete all steps, up to Presentation, preferably only an hour or so before serving. If preparing well in advance, cover with plastic wrap and refrigerate (because of the mayonnaise) until ready to serve. (Some of the flavor is lost through refrigeration.)

Curry Peas

A crisp, well-seasoned Indian snack, eaten like peanuts. In Nairobi, Kenya, whole curry peas are sold in small packets to school children at recess.

May be prepared in advance.

> 2 cups dried yellow split peas (1 pound)
> Water
> ½ teaspoon baking soda
> Oil for deep frying
> 2 teaspoons curry powder
> 1 teaspoon cayenne pepper
> 1 tablespoon coarse salt, or to taste*

1. Soak split peas overnight in cold water to cover with the baking soda.

2. Drain and dry well on paper toweling. Then put a handful at a time in a wire strainer and lower carefully into deep hot oil (375°). (It will bubble up rapidly.) Fry until the bubbling subsides considerably and the peas are golden and crisp (about 1½ minutes). Remove; drain and turn onto dry paper toweling to absorb excess oil.

3. Sprinkle with a mixture of the curry powder, cayenne pepper and salt. (This is hot; use less cayenne if desired.) When cool, store in a tightly covered container to keep fresh. The curry peas will keep at top quality at least 1 week. Reheat, if necessary, to crisp. Yield: about 4 cups.

PRESENTATION: Serve in small bowls as you would peanuts.

---

* Coarse salt is salt in large crystals. It is labeled and sold as kosher salt, and is available in many supermarkets.

Indian Dry Curry

This is real Indian curry, and requires rice and a variety of side dishes called *sambals* for authenticity. It is aromatic with spices but not fiery. The curry powder here (ground spices or *masala*) is of your own making, and much better than any purchased kind. A dry curry is one in which each piece of meat is barely covered with sauce, not swimming in it.

Should be prepared in advance.

- ½ pound butter, clarified (method below)
- 3 medium onions, finely chopped (3 cups)
- 6 cloves garlic, minced
- 1 tablespoon cumin seed
- Seeds from 24 whole cardamom pods*
- 1 tablespoon coriander seeds
- 1½ teaspoons peppercorns
- 1½ teaspoons ground cloves
- 1 teaspoon ground cinnamon
- ¼ teaspoon freshly grated nutmeg
- 2 teaspoons turmeric
- 2 tablespoons salt
- 5 pounds boneless lamb shoulder or leg, cut in 1-inch cubes and trimmed of excess fat
- 4 ripe tomatoes (1½ cups), skinned, seeded and coarsely chopped (see Index II for skinning method)

GARNISH:
Sprigs of fresh coriander or parsley

ACCOMPANIMENTS:
Sambals (recipes below)
Steamed Rice, Indian Style (recipe page 147)

---

* Cardamom is an expensive spice native to India. The tiny, black seeds, enclosed in a papery pod, are usually removed and ground before using and the pod discarded.

1. Heat about half of the clarified butter in a large Dutch oven. Add the finely chopped onions and minced garlic; sauté over low heat until golden, but not brown, about 10 minutes. Stir occasionally.

2. To make a curry powder, combine the cumin, cardamom seeds (removed from the pods) and coriander seeds with peppercorns in a mortar; crush with a pestle until pulverized (or use a blender). Add to onions along with the ground cloves, cinnamon, nutmeg, turmeric and salt. Sauté over low heat for 2 or 3 minutes, stirring constantly. (This is important as it brings out the oils in the spices.)

3. Add remaining clarified butter and meat cubes; mix lightly but thoroughly; cook over medium heat until most of the liquid has been absorbed by the meat and it has turned color, about 10 minutes. Stir occasionally to cook evenly.

4. Stir in the chopped tomatoes, cover and simmer 1¼ to 1½ hours, or until the meat is very tender. At this point it should be well glazed in a thick, rich sauce that barely covers each piece. Spoon off excess fat.

Note: It will be necessary to check the meat frequently to ensure it is cooking properly, not sticking to the pan. If it seems too dry, add a little water. If when the meat is tender there is too much liquid, remove the meat and cook sauce down to proper consistency.

5. Place, covered, in a 200° oven about 30 minutes before serving. This will keep the curry warm and improve the flavor. However, it is best made at least a day in advance.

PRESENTATION: Spoon onto a warm serving platter, large enough to hold the curry and rice, and garnish with sprigs of fresh coriander. Accompany with the Sambals, each served in an individual small bowl. Guests select from these, or take a little of each, to sprinkle on top of the curry. Traditionally the rice and dry curry are served side by side, not one on top of the other.

To prepare in advance: Complete steps 1 through 4, up to holding in the oven; cool, then refrigerate but bring to room temperature before reheating slowly. It may be necessary to sprinkle with more water to achieve the same consistency as when first prepared, as the meat will absorb some of the sauce. It is not necessary to use the oven procedure (step 5) when prepared in advance.

Sambals

Shredded Carrots: To 1½ cups finely shredded raw carrots add ½ teaspoon ground dry red chilies and 1 tablespoon lemon juice.

Chopped Fresh Tomatoes: Chop firm red tomatoes in ¼-inch cubes to make 2 cups. (With the salad in this menu, this sambal may be omitted.)

Sliced Bananas: Use small firm bananas, sliced into ¼-inch rounds, and sprinkled with lemon juice to keep them from turning brown. Do at last minute. Use 2 or 3 bananas.

Chopped Scallions: 1 medium bunch will do; use part of the green.

Sliced Chili Peppers: Thin rings of fresh green chilies; or use red or green canned ones preserved in vinegar (about 1 cup).

Coarsely Chopped Cashews: About 1 cup.

Sweet Mango Chutney: 1 jar of any brand. Major Grey is the easiest to find. Use about 1½ cups.

Hot Mango Pickle: 1 jar. This is found in foreign food shops. Sliced Mango Pickle bottled by M. M. Poonjiaji & Co. of Bombay is excellent. This particular sambal "makes" the curry for me. Use about 1½ cups.

Grated Coconut: Use canned, preferably unsweetened, if you can find it; about 1 cup.

CLARIFIED BUTTER

Foods sautéed in clarified butter have the flavor of butter and the added advantage of being sautéed without fear of burning, since the impurities are removed and only the pure golden fat remains.
May be prepared in advance.

Sweet butter (any quantity, but at least ¼ pound)

1. Cut butter in chunks and place in a heavy saucepan. Melt over medium-low heat, then turn heat to medium, and when butter bubbles, stir to mix well. When the bubbling turns to foam, remove from heat. There should be some light-brown sediment at the bottom, but the part above should be a rich golden color. (The whole process takes about 5 minutes.)
2. Let stand 5 minutes to settle, then skim any remaining foam from the top. (Use this to season vegetables if desired.) Carefully pour off the clear liquid butter into a screw-top jar, leaving the sediment at the bottom of the saucepan. Use immediately, or cover and store in the refrigerator. It will keep for weeks without turning rancid.

Note: To skip the clarification step, many foods are sautéed in a mixture of butter and oil; the oil allows the butter to reach a higher temperature without burning.

Steamed Rice, Indian Style

Many Indian cooks prefer to add lemon juice when steaming their rice. The acid helps keep it white. The cooked rice is dry and slightly chewy.
May be prepared in advance.

3 cups long-grain rice* (not converted)
3 cups cold water
3 teaspoons salt
2 teaspoons lemon juice

1. Measure rice and put into a 4-quart heavy saucepan. Wash, rubbing the rice through the fingers, in several changes of water until the water is almost clear. (This rids the rice of excess starch and prevents scorching when cooking.) Drain off water.

2. Add cold water in the same amount as rice (for this recipe 3 cups). Stir in the salt and lemon juice. Level the rice with your hand. Bring to a boil over high heat, then cover and reduce heat to as low as possible. Let the rice steam for 13 to 15 minutes. Do not remove the lid during this period. Rice is done when water is absorbed and rice is dry. (At the minimum cooking time, tip the pan to see if any water is remaining; if so, cook a minute or two longer.) Remove the pan from the heat, and let stand, covered, 15 minutes longer to complete the steaming process.

3. After this second steaming period, remove lid and stir with a fork to fluff and separate the grains. Yield: about 2½ quarts.

PRESENTATION: Serve hot, as an accompaniment to the Indian Dry Curry.

To prepare in advance: Complete step 1 a few hours in advance; be sure rice is well drained. Or, steam rice, turn into a casserole and cool. Reheat, loosely covered, in a 350° oven until heated through. Sprinkle a tablespoon or two of water over the top before reheating.

Tomato and Cucumber Salad, the Turkish Way

In Turkey, the arrangement of the foods and garnishes is as important as the quality of ingredients used. This salad is one fine example.

May be prepared in advance.

* Indian rice may be used for complete authenticity, but it is expensive. See Index I for Steamed Basmati Rice recipe.

⅔ cup olive oil
4 tablespoons lemon juice (2 lemons)
4 teaspoons salt
½ teaspoon freshly ground pepper
3 medium cucumbers
8 small tomatoes
1 cup coarsely chopped parsley (flat-leaf Italian preferred)

GARNISH:
A few thin lemon slices

1. To make the dressing, combine the oil, lemon juice, 1 tea-spoon of the salt and the pepper; beat with a fork to blend. Set aside.

2. Peel cucumbers with a vegetable peeler. Slice thinly across (⅛ inch) into a bowl, discarding the ends, which are often bit-ter. (Do not use a shredder as it cuts too thin.) Cover with cold water; add 3 teaspoons salt and mix with the fingers to distribute. Put a handful or two of ice cubes on top and let stand at least 1 hour to crisp. Replenish ice cubes as necessary.

3. Drain cucumbers in a colander. Arrange slices overlapping down one side of a large oval platter, leaving a space down the center.

4. Core tomatoes and cut in thin slices. Arrange overlapping down the other side of the platter. Put a bed of chopped parsley down the center. Pour dressing over all.

PRESENTATION: Garnish salad with a few lemon slices. Serve immediately.

To prepare in advance: Complete all steps, up to adding the dressing. Chill. When ready to serve, add the dressing and gar-nish.

Pappadums

Pappadums are as essential to curries as are *sambals*. They are paper-thin, crisp wafers the size of a small plate, somewhat similar to the Mexican fried tortilla, but much more delicate. The dough is made from lentil flour and spices, which give the pappadums an unusual but attractive flavor. Best of all, they are purchased ready-made and need only to be fried to crisp.

May be prepared in advance.

24 pappadums*
Oil for frying

1. Heat about 1 inch of oil in a 9- or 10-inch skillet, and when hot (about 375°), slip in 1 pappadum. It will expand immediately (pappadums double in diameter) and bubble irregularly. When it seems to have expanded to its limit (this takes only a few seconds), turn it over with tongs to fry on the other side and expose all areas to the oil. Remove as soon as it changes color and becomes crisp. Do not brown; it should be somewhat pale in color.

2. Drain, propped up on edge, on paper toweling; keep warm in a 200° oven and repeat with rest of pappadums, adding oil as necessary. They may appear oily, but if done in advance most of the oil will be absorbed before serving. Yield: 24 pappadums.

PRESENTATION: Serve warm as an accompaniment to the lamb curry, stacked high on a platter, wood, if you have one. To eat, a portion is broken off and eaten plain without butter.

To prepare in advance: Complete all steps; drain, cool and leave at room temperature. When ready to serve, reheat in a 250° oven a few minutes to crisp.

Note: If weather is dry and pappadums are made late in the afternoon, reheating is not absolutely necessary.

---

* Pappadums are imported in tins or cartons from India, where they are commercially made. The imported ones are dry, and they keep for months after package is opened, if it is resealed. They are available in stores specializing in Indian foods, or at other foreign food shops. Rajah brand is very good.

Fresh Pineapple, Bombay Style

Here is an unusual way of trimming and slicing a fresh pineapple with amazingly little waste. Even the core stays intact and
can be eaten if not too hard. This conservative method of cutting
has a built-in bonus: thin slices of pineapple with attractive
feathered edges that are the beginning of an easy dessert. All
you need to add is kirsch and black cherries, or other fresh fruit
in season.
Should be prepared in advance.

2 large, ripe pineapples with attractive leaf crowns
   Sugar, if necessary
   Kirsch, if desired
1 pound Bing cherries on the stem*

1. Cut off the leaf crown of each pineapple with an inch or so
of the pineapple intact. Reserve 1 crown.
2. Cut off base and discard. Stand on end, and with a sharp
knife pare off rind, cutting very close so as not to waste the fruit.
You will be left with pineapple full of "eyes," which wind
around the pineapple in a spiral. It is possible to remove the eyes
by cutting around the fruit, following the spiral, but for this
recipe the following method is necessary.
3. Place the pineapple on its side with the base toward you.
With a long sharp knife, cut out 3 or 4 "eyes" at a time (in a
vertical row), cutting a notchlike trough from the pineapple.
Continue until you have done this all the way around the pineapple, then go back for the leftover odd ones, but again cut vertically. If there are any areas without troughs cut into them, cut
notches in these too. The idea is to have somewhat "feathered"
edges when you slice the pineapple across.
4. With the pineapple still on its side, cut across in very thin

* The cherries are mainly a garnish. Any sweet cherry may be used. If not in
season, substitute fresh strawberries. Rinse, but leave hulls on if attractive. You
will need 1 pint.

slices, less than ¼ inch thick. Do not remove core. Repeat process
with remaining pineapple.

5. Place the reserved leaf crown in the center of a large serving
platter and arrange the pineapple slices, overlapping each other,
around it. Sprinkle lightly with sugar if not sweet enough.
Dribble kirsch to taste over the pineapple if desired. (A fully
ripe, sweet pineapple needs neither sugar nor kirsch.)

6. Rinse the cherries, leaving the stems on, and scatter over
the pineapple slices, some in the crown if you like. Chill until
serving time. For best flavor, the fruit should not be icy cold.

PRESENTATION: Place platter and dessert plates
on the buffet and invite guests to help themselves.

To prepare in advance: Complete all steps any time during the
day. You cannot hold the pineapple overnight if well ripened,
as once it is cut, decay is rapid. The fruit will turn translucent
in places and lose its juices.

MENU
BUFFET

FIRST COURSE: • *Champignons and Cheese*

MAIN COURSE: *Shrimp de Jonghe*
               • *Tomatoes Stuffed with Creamed Spinach*
               Caesar Salad, a Variation

DESSERT: *Cinnamon Cheesecake*
              Coffee

• Quick and Easy Recipe

Champignons and Cheese

The inspiration for this unusual appetizer comes from a restaurant in the tiny village of Chêne-Bourg just outside Geneva, Switzerland. The proprietor of the Café du Gothard described this creation simply as "mushrooms." These mushrooms are truly fresh; they are turned in oil but are not marinated. Marinated mushrooms take on a "cooked" quality not desirable in this recipe. There is a certain attractive earthiness to a really raw mushroom.

May be partially prepared in advance.

  1½ pounds fresh mushrooms (white and firm)
    6 ounces Swiss cheese (Emmenthal), cut in thin 1-
         by ⅛-inch squares
    ¼ cup very finely chopped parsley
    ½ cup walnut oil*

* Walnut oil is often used in salad dressings in France. It may be purchased in foreign and health food stores, and some supermarkets. It is mild with a subtle nut flavor. Salad oil may be substituted, but with a slightly different result. Walnut oil keeps for months without refrigeration but eventually will turn rancid. Use with delicate greens, either alone or in combination with any bland salad oil.

153

3 tablespoons lemon juice
1½ teaspoons salt

1. Cut stems from mushrooms at the base and use for another purpose. Wipe caps with a damp paper towel. Place caps stem side down and cut through in ⅛-inch slices. Quickly drop in cold salted water (2 teaspoons to 1 quart) to rinse and keep from discoloring. Remove immediately; do not soak as they absorb the water rapidly. Drain in a colander, then on paper toweling. The mushrooms will stay white for several hours.

2. Combine mushrooms with cheese and chopped parsley in a large salad bowl.

3. Combine the walnut oil, lemon juice and 1½ teaspoons salt. Pour over the mushrooms and cheese and toss to distribute evenly, using your hands to prevent bruising the mushrooms.

PRESENTATION: Serve immediately on a large platter and let guests help themselves. Provide small plates.

To prepare in advance: Complete steps 1 through part of 3, up to tossing the mushrooms and cheese with the dressing. Set aside, covered, at room temperature.

Shrimp de Jonghe

This famed combination of aromatic shrimp with sherried bread crumbs originated in Chicago in a restaurant run by the Belgian family de Jonghe. Though there are several versions of this recipe, to my knowledge the original recipe was never divulged.

May be partially prepared in advance.

4½ pounds raw medium shrimp
1 lemon, cut in quarters
5 or 6 parsley stems

   1 small onion, cut in quarters
  ½ pound butter, softened (1 cup)
  4 cloves garlic, put through a press
  ¼ cup chopped parsley
  1 teaspoon dried tarragon, crushed
  ¼ teaspoon cayenne pepper
1½ teaspoons salt
  ¾ cup dry sherry (good quality)
  3 to 3½ cups Fresh Bread Crumbs (method below)

GARNISH:
A few sprigs of parsley

1. Shell shrimp by pulling off legs, then body shell. To remove tail shell, push small hard piece above tail upward to break and remove. Carefully pull the tips of the tail. The shell should come off in one piece, leaving the tail flesh intact, if properly done. This turns a brilliant pink when cooked and enhances the appearance of the prepared dish.

Note: With some types of shrimp this is almost impossible to do; if it seems tedious, simply remove tail shell *with* flesh and discard.

Cut shrimp deeply down the back, lengthwise, to the tail. Remove vein with flat tip of the knife. (An easy way is to have a folded paper towel ready and wipe the vein on that; keep folding as it becomes soiled.) For best flavor do not rinse the shrimp unless particles of vein are left.

2. Put the shelled and deveined shrimp in a 6-quart saucepan and add water to come up about 1 inch above the shrimp. Add lemon quarters, parsley stems and onion. Bring the water to a boil (just), remove from heat and drain in a colander. The shrimp will be cooked through. Allow to cool. If not using immediately, cover to keep from drying out.

3. Blend together the softened butter, garlic, chopped parsley, tarragon, cayenne and salt. Gradually add the sherry and bread crumbs alternately, mixing thoroughly after each addition. The mixture should be somewhat crumbly; if too moist add more crumbs.

4. Arrange cooked shrimp in a buttered shallow casserole (about 3-quart capacity) no more than 2 or 3 deep. Top with the seasoned crumb mixture.

5. Bake uncovered on a rack set in highest position of a pre-heated 450° oven about 10 to 15 minutes, or until the shrimp are piping hot and crumbs are lightly browned. Do not overbake.

> PRESENTATION: Serve hot from the casserole. The golden crumbs and flecks of herbs are enhanced by the addition of a few sprigs of parsley.

To prepare in advance: Complete steps 1 through 4, up to baking the shrimp. Cover with plastic wrap, then with foil, and refrigerate, but bring to room temperature before baking.

FRESH BREAD CRUMBS

Trim crisp crusts from bread if using French or Italian (if bread has a soft crust, it may be left on if desired); break rest apart and whirl about ½ cup at a time in an electric blender to form tiny crumbs. Lacking a blender, cut in cubes and force through a coarse-meshed wire sieve (stale bread is best for this method). Crumbs keep well when frozen. Use directly from freezer; no need to thaw.

Tomatoes Stuffed with Creamed Spinach

Sometimes frozen foods really simplify the making of a dish without compromising its quality. This is an excellent example. *May be partially prepared in advance.*

> 10   medium tomatoes (ripe but firm), about 3 pounds
>   Salt
>   2   packages (9 ounces each) creamed spinach (frozen in the bag)
>   5   teaspoons grated Parmesan cheese

GARNISH:
Clusters of parsley

1. Slice off the top quarter from the stem end of each tomato, which includes the hard core; discard or use later in salad. Gently run an index finger around the inside of each to release the juices and force out the seeds. Salt lightly and turn upside down on a rack to drain. Let stand at least 1 hour.

2. Cook spinach according to package directions. Cool in the bags in cold water.

3. To fill tomatoes, cut the corner from each bag and squeeze spinach into tomatoes. Arrange in an oiled shallow baking dish (two 8-inch pie plates will hold 10 tomatoes) and sprinkle each with ½ teaspoon Parmesan cheese.

4. Bake in lower third of a preheated 450° oven for 10 to 15 minutes, or until heated through and bubbly.

PRESENTATION: Serve while hot directly from baking dish. Overhandling may make them split. Nestle clusters of parsley between tomatoes.

To prepare in advance: Complete steps 1 through 3, up to baking. This may be done a day in advance. Refrigerate, but bring to room temperature before baking.

Caesar Salad, a Variation

This salad is featured in many fine restaurants throughout the country. It is always expensive, invariably good. It can be made easily—if not quickly—at home. There are greens to crisp, garlic croutons to make, cheese to grate and eggs to cook briefly. These eggs are broken directly over the salad but blend with the dressing to make a light coating for each leaf. Caesar salad is usually made with only romaine lettuce and with anchovies. This variation includes a bitter green, chicory (also called curly endive), and omits the anchovy.

May be partially prepared in advance.

2 to 3 heads romaine lettuce, to make 2½ quarts torn greens
1 head chicory, to make ½ quart of torn greens
2 cups bread cubes (stale French or Italian bread is best—crusts removed and cut into ½-inch cubes)
¾ cup olive oil
2 cloves garlic, crushed with the flat of a knife
2 eggs, at room temperature
1 tablespoon lemon juice
1 tablespoon red wine vinegar
1 teaspoon salt
½ teaspoon freshly ground pepper
3 tablespoons freshly grated Parmesan cheese

1. Wash the greens; drain briefly. Tear into large bite-size pieces discarding cores and any browned edges. Drain in a colander, then roll up in one layer in a terry-cloth towel, turning ends under. Refrigerate in the towel for at least 1 hour to crisp; the towel will absorb any remaining moisture.

2. To make the croutons, heat ¼ cup of the olive oil in a medium-size heavy skillet. Add the crushed garlic cloves and sauté until golden. Remove and discard the garlic. Off heat, add the bread cubes, stirring rapidly with a fork to coat all sides. Turn the heat to low, place skillet over heat and continue stirring until the cubes are browned evenly. Drain on paper toweling. If not completely crisp and dry, place on a baking sheet and dry in a 250° oven. Let cool and set aside uncovered.

3. Just before serving, place greens in a bowl large enough for tossing easily. Add the remaining ½ cup oil and toss lightly to coat the greens.

4. Lower the eggs in the shell in boiling water and cook 1 minute only; cool under cold running water. Break the eggs directly over the greens; add the lemon juice, vinegar, salt and pepper. Toss again.

5. Add the grated Parmesan cheese; toss, taste and correct seasoning if necessary. Add the croutons just before serving, mixing lightly. Serve immediately.

PRESENTATION: This is one of those showman-ship salads, a good one to toss in front of guests if you are so inclined. Have greens in salad bowl and remaining ingredients close at hand. Serve it as a separate course.

To prepare in advance: Complete steps 1 and 2, up to tossing the salad, but also boil eggs in advance. If desired, wash greens 1 or 2 days ahead, store in the towel and refrigerate. Do not tear into bite-size pieces until the day of serving as they may brown and lose their crispness.

Cinnamon Cheesecake

This is no ordinary cheesecake, even though the filling is typical and the crust familiar. It is the topping that makes the difference—not only cinnamon, but sour cream and blanched almond halves in abundance.
Must be prepared in advance.

     Graham Cracker Crust (recipe below)
   1 pound cream cheese, softened at room temperature
1½ cups sugar
   3 eggs
1½ cups dairy sour cream (12-ounce carton)
   1 teaspoon vanilla extract
     Ground cinnamon
  30 almonds, blanched and halved* (method below)

1. Prepare and bake Graham Cracker Crust.
2. Beat the softened cream cheese until fluffy, using an electric beater. Beat in ½ cup of the sugar, then the eggs, one at a time. Beat only until smooth. Pour into prepared crust.
3. Bake in a preheated 350° oven for 15 to 20 mintes, or until firm in the center. Cool 10 minutes on a rack away from drafts.

* Do not use sliced almonds as they turn translucent when baked.

4. Combine sour cream with the 1 cup remaining sugar and the vanilla. Spoon the mixture gently over the slightly cooled cheesecake. Dust with cinnamon (use a fine wire sieve for even covering), and arrange the blanched almond halves, *flat side up*, over the entire top.

5. Return to the 350° oven and bake 10 minutes longer. Cool to room temperature on a rack. Then chill in the refrigerator before serving. Twelve to 24 hours of chilling improves the flavor.

> PRESENTATION: Remove the sides of springform pan, cut in wedges and serve cold.

GRAHAM CRACKER CRUST

    1⅓ cups graham cracker crumbs (20 squares)
    ½   cup butter, melted (1 stick)
    ¼   cup sugar

1. Place the graham cracker crumbs in a mixing bowl. Work in the melted butter and the sugar until well distributed. With the back of a spoon, press mixture onto the bottom only of a 9-inch springform pan with sides in place.

2. Bake in a preheated 350° oven for 5 minutes. Place on a rack to cool.

To blanch and halve almonds: Pour boiling water (to cover) over almonds. Let stand 3 minutes, then drain in a colander. Slip off skins by pinching between fingers. Then while still warm and softened, split in half by inserting a small, sharp knife into the large end to force the almond to split along the natural division. Spread out on paper toweling and let stand several hours to dry out and crisp.

MENU
BUFFET

FIRST COURSE: *Gougère, a Burgundian Pastry*
· *Cherry Tomatoes*
Dry Red Wine

MAIN COURSE: *Beef Bourguignon*
· *Buttered Frozen Peas, a New Way*
Fresh Green Salad with Herb Vinaigrette

DESSERT: *Chocolate Soufflé Roll*
Coffee

· Quick and Easy Recipe

Gougère, a Burgundian Pastry

A French pastry specialty, said to have originated in Burgundy. It can be served hot or cold. The more usual way is to serve it cold, and, as the Burgundians prefer, with a glass of red wine. The basic dough is *choux* paste (used for cream puffs, Napoleons and the like), with the addition of grated Swiss cheese. A simple but outstanding hors d'oeuvre.

May be prepared in advance.

¼ pound butter, cut into chunks
1 cup water
1 teaspoon salt
1 cup unsifted all-purpose flour
4 large eggs, at room temperature
1¼ cups coarsely grated imported Swiss cheese* (6 ounces)

* Jarlsberg Swiss-type cheese imported from Norway is delicious. Many supermarkets carry it now.

161

GLAZE:

Made by combining 1 egg yolk with 1 teaspoon
heavy cream and ⅛ teaspoon salt

GARNISH:

Clusters of parsley

1. Put butter, water and salt in a large, heavy saucepan. Bring
to a rolling boil over medium heat. Add the flour all at once; turn
heat to low and beat briskly with a wooden spoon until the mixture forms a ball and leaves the sides of the pan.

2. Remove from heat and beat in the eggs one at a time. (Do
not add the next egg until the last is completely incorporated.)
After the final egg is beaten in, the paste should look smooth
and waxy and fall slowly off the spoon.

3. Stir in 1 cup of the grated cheese. Let cool 5 minutes, or
until barely warm.

4. Grease two 9-inch pie plates and dust with flour; knock out
excess.

5. Using a large spoon and a rubber spatula, arrange egg-
shaped pieces (about 8) of the paste around the inside edge to
form a ring, leaving a 4-inch hole in the center. Make as even as
possible. Repeat circle in the second pan with remaining paste.

6. Brush tops with a mixture of the egg yolk, cream and salt.
(Do not let it drip down onto the pan as this will cause the
gougère to rise unevenly.) Sprinkle remaining ¼ cup grated
cheese over the tops.

7. Bake while barely warm in the middle of a preheated 425°
oven for 10 minutes; reduce heat to 375° (do not open oven
door) and bake 30 to 35 minutes longer, or until well puffed and
golden, crisp and dry on the outsides.

8. Remove and immediately pierce the sides with a sharp knife
in four or five places to let out the steam, and prevent the
gougère from becoming soggy. Let stand 5 minutes on cooling
racks. Yield: 2 pastry rings.

PRESENTATION: Place *gougère* on serving plates
with a cluster of parsley in the center of each ring. Cut

in small sections and pass to guests while warm. Encourage guests to drink dry Burgundy with this instead of cocktails.

Note: If preferred, the *gougère* may be served just as it has cooled to room temperature, in the Burgundian manner, but it is best when eaten while warm.

To prepare in advance: To serve warm, complete all steps, cool; then reheat briefly (about 10 minutes) in a 350° oven. Or wrap in plastic bags and freeze. Thaw in bags before reheating.

Cherry Tomatoes

A simple addition to the appetizer course. The flavor goes well with *gougère*.
May be prepared in advance.

1 pint cherry tomatoes

Rinse tomatoes but leave stem ends on.

PRESENTATION: Serve at room temperature in a large bowl; pass or put in several small bowls and set around the room before guests arrive.

Beef Bourguignon

This is one of the truly great dishes of the world. Like many dishes made with wine, it is even better when reheated and served the following day.
Should be partially prepared in advance.

  4 pounds beef chuck or round, cut in 1- to 1½-inch
     cubes
  ½ cup flour plus 2 tablespoons
  4 tablespoons butter
  4 tablespoons oil
  2 ounces brandy, heated until hot (¼ cup)
2½ cups red Burgundy wine
1½ teaspoons salt
  ½ teaspoon freshly ground pepper
  2 small bay leaves
  2 cloves garlic, put through a garlic press
  ½ cup chopped fresh parsley
  1 teaspoon dry thyme
  1 can (10½ ounces) beef consommé (undiluted) and
     water to make 3 cups liquid
30 small white onions, cooked (method below)
  1 pound fresh mushrooms, sautéed (method below)

GARNISH:
Chopped parsley

1. Roll beef cubes in the flour. Heat a heavy saucepan or Dutch oven over medium heat. Add butter and oil. Start with 2 tablespoons of each and add as needed. When fat is hot, sauté beef cubes a few at a time until browned on all sides. (Do not crowd the meat.) Remove pieces as they are browned and set aside. Repeat process with remaining beef, adding more butter and oil as necessary. If any flour is left, add to pan and cook and stir 1 minute until golden.

2. When all beef cubes are browned, return to the pan. Add the heated brandy and light a match to it. (The secret to flaming is hot brandy and hot beef.) When the flame dies down, add a little of the wine and stir up browned drippings sticking to the pan. Add remaining wine (reserving ½ cup), salt, pepper, bay leaves, garlic, parsley and thyme. Add the can of consommé and enough water to make 3 cups in all.

3. Simmer, uncovered, 1½ to 2 hours, or until meat is tender. The meat is done when a fork pierces it easily. The sauce should

be thick enough to coat a spoon lightly. If too thin, remove meat
and boil sauce down rapidly. If too thick, add a little water and
simmer 5 minutes. Taste and correct seasoning if necessary.

4. Add the cooked onions and sautéed mushrooms. Baste with
the sauce. Cover and cook 5 minutes longer, or until very hot.
Stir in the reserved ½ cup Burgundy just before serving.

PRESENTATION: Turn into a heated serving
dish and sprinkle with chopped parsley.

To prepare in advance: Complete steps 1 through 3, up to
adding the mushrooms and onions. Cool, then refrigerate. Prepare
mushrooms and onions, if you wish, and store separately. Cover
and refrigerate these if prepared a day in advance. To serve, reheat beef slowly, then add mushrooms and onions. When hot,
add the remaining ½ cup wine.

Note: Before reheating it may be necessary to sprinkle with
more water to achieve the same consistency as when first prepared, as the meat will absorb some of the sauce.

To prepare onions: Drop unpeeled onions into boiling water;
return to a boil, then simmer a few seconds to loosen skins. Drain
and peel. Trim and cut a small deep cross in the root end with
the point of a small knife, to prevent bursting while cooking.
Then brown in a large skillet in 2 tablespoons butter with ½
teaspoon of sugar added. Add a little water and ½ teaspoon salt.
Cover and steam until tender, about 20 to 30 minutes, depending
on size.

To prepare mushrooms: Wipe mushrooms and trim ends. If
small, leave whole. If large, remove stems and cut these in 2 or 3
pieces; quarter caps. Heat 2 tablespoons butter and 1 tablespoon
oil in a large skillet. When foam subsides, add half the mushrooms
and sauté over high heat 4 to 5 minutes, or until lightly browned.
Shake pan often. Repeat with remaining mushrooms, adding
small amounts of butter and oil.

Buttered Frozen Peas, a New Way

This method of cooking frozen peas ensures peas that are bright green, firm and almost as good as those fresh from the pod. *May be prepared in advance.*

3 packages (10-ounce size) frozen green peas
6 tablespoons sweet butter
Salt to taste

1. Remove peas from packages and put in a colander. Run cold water over them to separate.
2. While still frozen, drop into a saucepan filled with 6 quarts of unsalted boiling water. When the water boils and all the peas come bouncing to the top, they are done. (This will take only a few minutes.) Pour into a colander to drain.
3. Melt butter slowly in a large skillet; add the hot peas and carefully turn to coat. Salt to taste and turn again. Let stand in the skillet a minute or two to be certain the peas are really hot. Taste and be certain they are cooked through.

PRESENTATION: Turn into a heated serving bowl, which may be held in a 200° oven, covered, up to 10 minutes. (The peas must remain moist to keep from wrinkling.)

To prepare in advance: Complete steps 1 and 2, up to coating with butter. Cool under running water; drain. Reheat a few minutes in the melted butter when ready to serve.

Fresh Green Salad with Herb Vinaigrette

A variety of fresh greens always makes an interesting tossed salad. This one contains 5.
May be partially prepared in advance.

Romaine, escarole, chicory (curly endive), Boston
    lettuce and iceberg lettuce—enough mixed greens
    to make 3 ½ quarts coarsely torn leaves
⅔ cup vegetable oil (use part olive oil)
3 ½ tablespoons red wine vinegar
 1 teaspoon salt
 ½ teaspoon freshly ground pepper
 ¼ teaspoon marjoram (scant)
 ¼ teaspoon thyme (scant)
 ¼ teaspoon basil (scant)
 1 clove garlic, crushed with the flat of a knife

1. Wash the greens, except iceberg lettuce, in a sink filled with cold water. Discard cores and any bruised leaves. Drain briefly. Tear into large bite-size pieces. Then roll up in 1 layer in a terry-cloth towel, turning ends under. Refrigerate in the towel, which will absorb any remaining moisture. Store in the refrigerator at least 1 hour to crisp. (The iceberg lettuce does not need washing, but do not tear until up to an hour before serving as the edges may "rust.")

2. To make the salad dressing, measure the oil, vinegar, salt, pepper, marjoram, thyme, basil and crushed garlic into a screw-top jar. Cover and shake to blend the seasonings. Set aside at least 1 hour to blend the flavors. Remove the garlic just before mixing with the greens.

3. When ready to serve, place the mixed greens in a salad bowl large enough to toss the salad easily. Shake the dressing. Dribble it over the salad greens. Toss gently but thoroughly so leaves are well coated.

PRESENTATION: Serve immediately from salad bowl.

To prepare in advance: Complete steps 1 and 2, up to adding the dressing and tossing the salad. If preferred, wash greens 1 or 2 days in advance and store in a towel in the refrigerator. Tear into pieces the day of serving. The dressing may be made hours in advance.

Chocolate Soufflé Roll

A cake roll that is not actually cake, but a fallen soufflé. Filled with whipped cream, it makes a delicious dessert and perfection for chocolate lovers. It is easily made in spite of the lengthy directions.

Must be prepared in advance.

        8 squares (1 ounce each) semisweet chocolate
        5 tablespoons water
        4 large eggs, separated (at room temperature)
        1 cup sugar
          Whipped Cream Filling (recipe below)

        GARNISH:
        Dry cocoa
        Crushed pistachios (3 tablespoons) (method below)

1. Melt the chocolate with the water in a heavy, medium skillet over *very low* heat. Stir to melt evenly. Remove from heat, stir and set aside to cool slightly.

2. Beat egg yolks until thick and pale. (When the beater is lifted, the mixture should fall in a ribbon.) Add sugar gradually and beat until creamy. Stir in the melted chocolate.

3. Beat egg whites until stiff but not dry. Stir about ⅓ of the whites into the chocolate mixture to lighten it, then fold in the remainder until no white traces remain.

4. Oil a 15½-by-11-inch jelly-roll pan and place a sheet of wax paper in the pan. (It should be long enough to extend slightly above the ends about 1 inch.) Do not oil the paper.

5. Pour the batter into the prepared pan and spread it evenly. Bake in the middle of a preheated 350° oven for 15 to 17 minutes. (It will puff up and lose its gloss when done. Check at minimum time; do not overbake.)

6. Remove to a cooling rack. Immediately cover with a double thickness of wet paper toweling, wrung out. Then cover with a dry tea towel. Let cool to room temperature. (At this point, if

you prefer, it may be refrigerated overnight; bring to room temperature before proceeding with step 7.)

Note: The unusual method of cooling the cake (which keeps it from drying), and the following procedure for rolling, have been adapted from a technique created by the late Dione Lucas, who taught this method at her Gourmet Cooking School in New York.

7. Remove cloth towel and paper toweling. Shake cocoa through a sieve over the top. Turn cake out, long side toward you, onto two overlapping sheets of waxed paper, the one closest to you on top. (These should each be 20 inches long.) Carefully peel the waxed paper off the bottom of the cake.

8. Spread the Whipped Cream Filling evenly over the cake. With fingers under the wax paper, roll up like a jelly roll, removing and discarding sheet closest to you. If cake is cracked, sprinkle with additional cocoa. Wrap in second sheet of waxed paper, twisting ends to secure. Refrigerate until ready to serve, at least 1 hour, but up to 12 if preferred.

> PRESENTATION: Leave on wax paper and lift onto a serving platter or long jelly-roll board. Unwrap and trim paper close to cake on one side, then gently pull remaining paper from under cake. Cut in 1½-inch slices and sprinkle each portion with crushed pistachios.

To crush pistachios: Crush pistachios coarsely by pressing with flat of knife and pounding lightly with your fist. Pick over and discard the loose skins.

WHIPPED CREAM FILLING

    1½ cups heavy cream
      3 tablespoons confectioners' sugar, put through a sieve
      2 teaspoons vanilla extract

Pour cream into a mixing bowl and set in a bowl half-filled with ice. Whip the cream until slightly thickened. Add the sugar and vanilla and beat until stiff but not buttery.

Note: The use of confectioners' sugar (which contains cornstarch), and whipping the cream over ice, permits filling the roll hours in advance without the cream separating and turning the cake soggy.

Menus and Recipes for Twelve

MENU
BUFFET

FIRST COURSE: *Pickled Shrimp, Texas Style*
Heated Oyster Crackers

MAIN COURSE: *Tamale Pie*
· Refried Beans with Sour Cream
· Savoy Cabbage Salad
Crisp Tortillas
Beer

DESSERT: *Rum Pie*
Coffee

· Quick and Easy Recipe

Pickled Shrimp, Texas Style

Texans, especially, are addicted to marinated shrimp, but the enthusiasm for these is spreading. They are a great success at cocktail parties, and easy to eat (the shrimp are speared out of their marinade with picks). Best of all, the entire recipe can be prepared 3 days in advance.
Must be prepared in advance.

2½ pounds medium, raw shrimp
6 cups water
1 tablespoon whole pickling spices, in a tea ball* or
tied in a cheesecloth bag
3 small onions, thinly sliced and separated into rings
1½ lemons, thinly sliced
3 tablespoons capers (with juice)

* A tea ball (or tea egg) is a perforated metal container sometimes used when steeping tea to contain the loose tea leaves. It has a chain and hook for easy retrieval. I find it a useful container for spices and less trouble than cheesecloth, which (incidentally) should be rinsed before using to remove the "sizing."

173

⅓ cup chopped parsley
3 small bay leaves
1⅛ cups vegetable oil
¾ cup white vinegar
6 tablespoons lemon juice
2 teaspoons coarse salt
¼ teaspoon Tabasco sauce
1½ teaspoons dried tarragon, crushed

ACCOMPANIMENT:
Heated oyster crackers (optional)

1. Shell shrimp by pulling off legs, then body shell. To remove tail shell, push small hard pointed piece above tail upward to break and remove. Carefully pull the tips of tail shell. It should come off in one piece, leaving the tail flesh intact if properly done. (The tail turns a brilliant pink when cooked and makes the shrimp more attractive.)

Note: With some varieties this is almost an impossible task; if the process seems difficult, simply remove tail shell *with* flesh and discard.

Make a deep cut lengthwise down the back, and with the flat tip of a small knife remove the vein. Do not rinse unless the vein has been difficult to remove.

2. Bring the water and pickling spices to a boil, then turn to simmer and cook 5 minutes. Discard spices. Stir in shrimp and when water reaches the simmer, cook 2 to 3 minutes, stirring occasionally to keep the shrimp from sticking together. The shrimp are done when the tails curl up and the shrimp turn pink. Drain in a colander, then rinse with cold water to cool (preventing overcooking from the heat remaining).

3. Layer the shrimp in a non-metal bowl with onion rings, lemon slices, capers and parsley. Tuck in bay leaves.

4. Make marinade by combining oil, vinegar, lemon juice, salt, Tabasco and tarragon. Pour over the shrimp. Cover and refrigerate overnight (may, however, be prepared 3 days in advance). Turn occasionally if marinade does not cover shrimp completely.

PRESENTATION: Serve chilled, but not icy cold, in the marinade in a large glass bowl. Supply picks for spearing (and cocktail napkins). Heated oyster crackers are very good with this.

Tamale Pie

Versions of this delicious casserole appear all over the Southwest. Here the "mush" is made from quick-cooking grits, which form a crust for the spicy chili filling. Slices of ripe olives give it added flavor, and sliced tomatoes are a colorful garnish.
May be partially prepared in advance.

      1 tablespoon lard or bacon drippings
      2 cups chopped onions
      3 cloves garlic, minced
      2 pounds ground beef chuck
   1¼ pounds lean pork, cut in ¼-inch cubes
      1 cup chopped green pepper
   1½ cups drained, canned tomatoes
      3 tablespoons chili powder
      2 teaspoons oregano, crushed
      1 teaspoon ground or crushed cumin seed
      1 tablespoon coarse salt
      1 cup pitted ripe olives, sliced across in thick rings
      8 cups water
      2 teaspoons salt
      2 chicken bouillon cubes
   2½ cups white hominy grits (quick-cooking type)
      4 tablespoons butter, cut in chunks (½ stick)
     ⅓ cup chopped parsley

   GARNISH:
   Thick, small tomato slices (at least 10)
   Grated Parmesan cheese (⅓ cup)
   Chopped parsley

1. Heat the lard in a large skillet or Dutch oven. Sauté the onions and garlic slowly until translucent. Add the ground beef and diced pork, stirring with a fork to break up fine. Sauté about 10 minutes or until very dry.

2. Stir in the chopped green pepper, drained tomatoes, broken up, chili powder, oregano, cumin seed and salt. Simmer over medium heat, stirring frequently until all the liquid has been absorbed, about 20 minutes. Remove from heat, tip skillet and spoon off excess fat. Stir in olive slices. Set aside.

3. Bring the 8 cups water to a boil in a heavy 4-quart saucepan. Add the salt and the chicken bouillon cubes. Slowly stir in the grits and return to a boil, then reduce heat and cook about 5 minutes, stirring occasionally. The mixture should be fairly dry. Add the butter and parsley; stir with a fork to distribute evenly until butter is melted.

4. Grease 2 shallow casseroles (1½-quart capacity each). Add about ⅔ of the grit mixture, dividing between the casseroles to line them evenly. Spoon in the meat mixture. Edge the top with the remaining grits, leaving the center open.

5. Bake in a preheated 350° oven for 35 minutes. Remove from oven and garnish the center with tomato slices. Sprinkle tomatoes and grits with grated cheese and bake 10 minutes longer, 45 minutes in all.

PRESENTATION: Serve hot from casseroles, sprinkled with a little chopped parsley for extra color.

To prepare in advance: Complete steps 1 through 4, up to baking, and allow casseroles to cool to room temperature. Bake an additional 10 minutes before adding sliced tomatoes and cheese.

Note: Long standing improves the flavor. If preferred, make a day in advance and refrigerate, but bring to room temperature before baking; or freeze, then thaw, to room temperature.

Refried Beans with Sour Cream

Refried beans are sautéed in lard or bacon drippings and mashed down during the cooking to absorb the fat and juices. Some manufacturers do the work for you and put the purée in cans. If you have the time, do your own, starting with canned whole beans. When mashing, leave a few beans whole to show you did it yourself. But for a menu for 12, you need all the assist possible, and therefore canned refried beans are recommended. The chilled sour cream is a cooling contrast to the bubbling hot beans. Tiny black beans and chopped scallions are added for color and texture.

> 2 tablespoons bacon drippings
> 4 cans (1-pound size) Mexican refried beans
> 1 can (1 pound) black beans*
> 1 pint dairy sour cream
>
> GARNISH:
> Chopped scallions

1. Melt bacon drippings in a medium-size skillet. Add refried beans and spread evenly. Cover and place over low heat until bubbling, about 15 minutes.
2. Warm black beans in their broth until hot; drain.

PRESENTATION: Spread refried beans on 1 or 2 heated serving plates. Spoon cold sour cream directly from carton onto beans and spread in center. Top with drained black beans, allowing a few to spill over sides of cream. Sprinkle with a few chopped scallions. Serve immediately.

* Black beans are available in Puerto Rican and Spanish stores, if not in your supermarket. If you cannot find them use an additional can of refried beans instead. The black beans are mainly for color.

Savoy Cabbage Salad

Savoy cabbage differs from other cabbage. It is more delicate in flavor and texture, and has attractive yellow-to-green crinkled leaves. Here it is shredded and marinated in a tangy dressing that brings out its gentle flavor. The cabbage shreds remain crisp even after hours in the marinade. The salad can stand as a centerpiece on the table if the giant outside leaves are used to line the salad bowl.

Should be prepared in advance.

1 to 2 heads Savoy cabbage (to make 3 quarts shredded cabbage)
2 tablespoons white or cider vinegar
¼ cup lemon juice (bottled is fine)
2 teaspoons dry mustard
¼ teaspoon monosodium glutamate
3 teaspoons salt
1 cup vegetable oil

SERVING CONTAINER:
Outside cabbage leaves (optional)

1. Remove any tough outer leaves of cabbage (see *Note* below). Cut cabbage in half and remove core. Using a heavy chef's knife, shred enough cabbage (¼- to ½-inch shreds) to make 3 quarts, packed. Cut any long shreds into bite-size pieces. Rinse with water and drain thoroughly. Refrigerate to crisp, at least ½ hour.

2. To make the marinade, pour the vinegar and lemon juice into a bowl large enough to allow for tossing. Add the dry mustard, monosodium glutamate and salt; beat with a fork to blend. Then beat in oil.

3. Add the shredded cabbage to the marinade and toss well. Let stand in a cool place at least 1 hour, mixing occasionally. If kept longer (up to 4 hours), refrigerate, but remove ½ hour before serving. It should be cool and crisp, not icy cold.

PRESENTATION: Serve from a large salad bowl.
No garnish is necessary as the green Savoy cabbage is
colorful enough alone.

Note: If the cabbage is purchased with the large outside leaves
intact, and if they are attractive, use these to line the salad bowl
for an unusual serving container. Supermarkets usually trim off
these leaves before selling. A fresh fruit and vegetable market
does not.

Crisp Tortillas

In Mexico these are referred to as *tostados*, or fried tortillas.
They are served whole but broken into smaller pieces before they
are eaten. (They make excellent scoops for eating the refried
beans.) The tortillas may be purchased in cans or frozen. The
frozen are a much better quality, and are recommended here. If
the canned ones must be substituted, follow the same procedure
for frying.
May be prepared in advance.

> 24 frozen tortillas, defrosted in package
> Oil for frying

1. Dry defrosted tortillas on paper toweling, if wet, but re-
stack to keep from drying out.
2. Heat about 1 inch of oil in a small heavy skillet (I prefer the
iron kind—6½-inches in diameter) over medium heat until very
hot, but not smoking. Slip in a tortilla; fry a few seconds on one
side; turn with tongs and fry on other side until it changes color
slightly; turn again just before removing. Drain on paper toweling. (The tortilla should be light in color, dry and crisp. If somewhat translucent, the fat was not hot enough; if dark and it fried
too quickly with the fat sputtering uncontrollably, the heat was
too high.) Repeat with remaining tortillas. Yield: 24 tortillas.

Note: I find that once the proper temperature is reached, it stays that way through the entire cooking procedure. For this number of tortillas, 2 skillets are preferable, but the procedure remains the same.

PRESENTATION: Serve warm from a napkin-lined basket.

To prepare in advance: Fry any time, even the day before, and when cooled, store in a plastic bag at room temperature. When ready to serve, recrisp in an oven set at any temperature between 300° and 400°.

Rum Pie

The smooth texture of this pie is one of its pleasures; the light rum flavor is another.

Must be prepared in advance.

2 teaspoons unflavored gelatin (⅔ package)
2 tablespoons cold water
1 cup sugar
¼ teaspoon salt
2 tablespoons cornstarch
6 egg yolks (unbeaten)
½ cup light rum
1 pint heavy cream, lightly whipped
2 Baked Pastry Shells (recipe below)

GARNISH:
Freshly grated nutmeg

1. Sprinkle the gelatin over the cold water in a medium saucepan. When softened, add the sugar, salt, cornstarch and egg yolks. Stir to blend.

2. Heat over low heat, stirring constantly, until sugar and gelatin dissolve and the mixture thickens. Do not boil.

3. Remove from heat; let cool 5 minutes, then stir in the rum. Pour into a bowl and chill until the mixture is cooled, but not jelled.

4. Stir in a little of the whipped cream to lighten the mixture, then fold in remainder. Turn into the two Baked Pastry Shells. Grate nutmeg lightly over the top. Chill at least 1 hour but no longer than 12, as the crust should remain crisp. (The closer to serving time the pie is made, the better it will be.) Yield: 2 8-inch pies.

PRESENTATION: Cut each pie in 6 wedges. Serve on dessert plates.

BAKED PASTRY SHELLS

2 ¼ cups sifted all-purpose flour
1 teaspoon salt
¾ cup vegetable shortening
6 tablespoons cold water (about)

1. Combine the flour and the salt in a mixing bowl. Cut in the shortening with a pastry blender until part of it looks like coarse cornmeal; the rest should be the size of small peas. Sprinkle water over the mixture, a tablespoon at a time, and mix lightly with a fork until all the flour is moistened. Gather dough into a ball, then divide into 2 balls.

2. Roll 1 ball out on a lightly floured board ⅛ inch thick and about 1½ inches larger in diameter than an 8-inch pie plate. Transfer to pie plate; trim edges to ½-inch overhang, fold under and flute to make an attractive edge. Repeat with remaining dough.

3. Prick pastry generously on bottom and sides with a fork. Bake shells in a preheated 400° oven for 10 to 12 minutes. (After about 5 minutes' baking, peek in oven and if shells are puffing in center, prick once or twice with a fork to release air and allow dough to settle.) Cool completely on cooling racks before filling.

To prepare in advance: The pastry may be prepared up to step 3, then placed into plastic bags and refrigerated for a day or two before baking. Bring to room temperature before pricking with a fork and placing in the oven.

MENU
BUFFET

FIRST COURSE:
- *Taramasalata*
  Assorted Unsalted Crackers
- *Hot Artichoke Appetizers*

MAIN COURSE:
  Moussaka in the Greek Manner
- *Greek Island Salad*
  Toasted Syrian Bread, Two Ways

DESSERT:
  Cheesecake with Pineapple Glaze
  Coffee

- Quick and Easy Recipe

Taramasalata

A Greek appetizer-salad, subtle in flavor, pale salmon in color. It is often eaten as a salad, served with crusty bread, but here it is spread on unsalted crackers. A ring of briny Greek olives provides the sole garnish. The taramasalata is quickly made in a blender.
Must be prepared in advance.

½ cup tarama (5 ounces)*
1 slice onion, chopped (about 1 tablespoon)
6 tablespoons fresh lemon juice (use 3 lemons)
3 slices white bread, crusts removed, soaked in water
     and squeezed dry
1½ cups olive oil (or part vegetable oil)

* Tarama is tiny carp roe, bright orange in color, which can be bought in jars or in bulk at a Greek grocery or specialty food store. Pack any unused portion into a jar and cover with a film of oil to preserve; refrigerate.

GARNISH:
Greek black olives

ACCOMPANIMENT:
Assorted unsalted crackers

1. Put the tarama, onion, lemon juice and crustless bread into the container of an electric blender. Add ¼ cup of the olive oil; blend a few seconds.

2. Turn blender to low and slowly add the remaining olive oil, almost drop by drop at first. When thick and creamy, like mayonnaise, stop motor and remove. (You may not be able to add all the oil.)

3. Pour into a shallow 1-quart bowl (glass preferable). Chill until ready to serve. (May be made several days in advance.) Yield: about 3 cups.

PRESENTATION: Ring the edge with a row of Greek olives set on end. Serve as a spread on unsalted crackers.

Hot Artichoke Appetizers

Pale green and pretty.
May be partially prepared in advance.

  1 can (14 ounces) artichoke hearts (10 to 12 count),
       drained and cut in thirds
36 rye melba rounds(purchased)
 ¼ pound butter
  1 clove garlic, crushed with the flat of a knife
    Sesame seeds
    Salt

1. Arrange melba rounds in a single layer in shallow ovenproof serving platters if possible. Otherwise use a jelly-roll pan. Put ⅓ artichoke heart on each round, cut side up.

2. Melt butter in a heavy 2-quart saucepan over low heat; add the garlic. Shake the pan until the moisture has cooked away and the butter begins to turn brown. (At first it will bubble and crackle, then subside just before turning color.) Remove from heat and discard garlic.

3. Dribble hot browned butter over artichokes and bread. Sprinkle lightly with sesame seeds. Season lightly with salt. Set aside until ready to serve.

4. Bake in a preheated 350° oven for 10 minutes, or until hot and bubbly. Yield: 30 to 36 appetizers.

PRESENTATION: Pass hot from baking dishes, but cool a minute or two for easier handling; or if using a jelly-roll pan, transfer to serving plates and serve immediately.

To prepare in advance: Complete steps 1 through 3, up to baking the appetizers.

Moussaka in the Greek Manner

Moussaka (the accent is on the last syllable) is a mixture of ground beef or lamb, tomato and eggplant, intriguingly seasoned, under a thick ricotta cheese crust. The combination is a staple in several of the Mideast countries. This version is only one of the ways they serve it in Greece.
May be prepared in advance.

   3 large eggplants (1½ pounds each)
   1 cup clarified butter (see Index II)
   3 medium onions, finely chopped (3 cups)
   3 cloves garlic, put through a press
   3 pounds ground beef chuck
1½ cans (8-ounce size) tomato sauce
  ½ cup dry red wine
  ¼ cup water

1½ teaspoons ground allspice
1½ teaspoons ground cumin seed
¾ teaspoon ground cinnamon
⅛ teaspoon ground cloves
1 tablespoon salt
6 dried hot red peppers, left whole
¾ cup chopped parsley (lightly packed)
1½ cups fine dry bread crumbs
1½ cups freshly grated Parmesan cheese (about 6
    ounces)
¾ cup butter (1½ sticks)
½ cup flour
6 cups milk, heated until very hot
6 eggs, beaten until frothy
1 teaspoon freshly grated nutmeg
2 cartons (15-ounce size) ricotta cheese

GARNISH:
Chopped parsley

1. Wash eggplant; do not peel. Trim off ends and discard; cut remainder across into slices ½ inch thick. Put in a colander and sprinkle with 2 tablespoons salt, let drain 30 minutes, then blot dry on paper toweling (this process will remove some of the bitter juices).

2. Using ¾ cup in all, heat a little of the clarified butter in a large skillet. Quickly sauté the eggplant slices, a few at a time, until lightly browned on both sides, adding more butter as needed. (The eggplant will absorb the fat quickly but will release some of it as it starts to brown.) Two skillets will ease the browning process.

3. In one of the same skillets, add the remaining ¼ cup butter and slowly sauté the onions and garlic until translucent. Add the ground beef, stirring with a fork to break up fine. Sauté about 10 minutes, or until well browned.

4. Stir in tomato sauce, wine, water, allspice, cumin seed, cinnamon, cloves, salt, hot peppers and parsley. Cook over medium heat, stirring frequently, until all the liquid has been absorbed,

about 15 minutes. Remove from heat and discard hot peppers. Spoon off excess fat.

5. Butter 2 shallow casseroles with total capacity of 6 quarts. Dust the bottoms lightly with a few of the bread crumbs.

6. Arrange alternating layers of eggplant and meat sauce in the casseroles, sprinkling each layer with Parmesan and crumbs (divide equally between the 2 casseroles). Set aside.

7. Make a custard sauce by melting the ¾ cup butter in a 4-quart saucepan and blending in the flour, stirring with a wooden spoon. Let bubble a minute or two to cook the flour, but do not let it brown. Gradually add the hot milk, stirring constantly, until thickened and smooth; remove from heat.

Dribble about 2 cups of the hot sauce into the beaten eggs, stirring constantly. Add to remaining sauce. Cook gently 2 or 3 minutes longer, stirring constantly. Remove from heat. (The sauce must not boil or the eggs will curdle.) Stir in ricotta and nutmeg. Cool slightly.

8. Pour custard sauce over eggplant and beef in the casseroles.

9. Bake uncovered in a preheated 375° oven for 50 to 60 minutes, or until casseroles are bubbling and tops are an *uneven* golden brown. (Switch casseroles if baking on two levels to heat evenly.)

PRESENTATION: Let stand at room temperature about 20 minutes, to cool somewhat for easier serving. It is best served warm, not piping hot. Sprinkle with chopped parsley. Cut in squares, or have guests spoon out servings.

To prepare in advance: Complete steps 1 through 8, up to baking the casseroles. Cool and refrigerate (a day in advance for best flavor). Bring to room temperature before baking for accurate timing. Or, bake a day in advance, refrigerate and reheat to warm when ready to serve. Although traditionally done this way, the former is better, as the dish is less dry.

Greek Island Salad

This is a colorful salad of pale green cucumber chunks, bright red tomatoes, black olives and chalk-white goat cheese (feta). On the Greek isles, a slab of this salty cheese tops an individual salad. For buffets, to serve in one bowl, it is preferable to crumble it.

May be prepared in advance.

> 8 firm medium tomatoes (preferably homegrown)
> 4 medium cucumbers
> 24 Greek black olives
> 12 ounces Greek feta cheese,* coarsely crumbled
>   Mint Dressing (recipe below)

1. Core and cut each tomato in 6 to 8 wedges. Peel cucumbers with a vegetable peeler, discard ends and cut in quarters lengthwise, then in 1-inch chunks. Combine tomatoes and cucumbers; chill.

2. Place tomatoes and cucumbers in a salad bowl. Toss with Mint Dressing. Add olives and cheese and toss just enough to distribute.

PRESENTATION: Serve in salad bowl with salad servers.

To prepare in advance: Complete step 1, up to tossing the salad, and make the dressing. The salad may be tossed up to ½ hour before serving; longer, the dressing will draw the juices from the tomatoes. They should be firm and fresh-tasting.

* Feta is a crumbly dry goat cheese from Greece which is preserved in a salty brine. It can be purchased mild, medium or sharp, in the bulk, at Greek groceries. There are a Danish-made feta, put up in tins in brine, and a dry Wisconsin-made variety. Both are mild, acceptable, but not as good as the Greek. Supermarkets carry these.

MINT DRESSING

> ¾ cup olive oil (Greek preferred)
> 4 tablespoons red wine vinegar
> 1 tablespoon dried mint leaves, crushed
> 1½ teaspoons dried oregano, crushed
> 1 teaspoon salt
> ¼ teaspoon freshly ground pepper

Combine oil, vinegar, mint, oregano, salt and pepper; beat with a fork to blend.

Toasted Syrian Bread, Two Ways

Syrian or Middle Eastern bread, also called *pita*, is popular in several of the Middle Eastern countries. This bread is unleavened and traditionally baked with an air pocket inside. It is often cut and filled like a sandwich. Here the loaves are split, fragrantly seasoned and lightly toasted.

May be partially prepared in advance.

> 8 rounds Middle Eastern flat bread,* cut in half and
>   split open
> 6 teaspoons lemon juice
> 1 cup butter, softened (½ pound)
> 2 tablespoons chopped parsley
> 4 teaspoons thyme
> 2 tablespoons sesame seeds

1. Sprinkle soft cut sides of bread slices with lemon juice, then spread with softened butter.

---

* Middle Eastern flat bread can be bought fresh in Greek or Syrian markets (often with sesame seeds). Sahara brand, made in Massachusetts, is widely distributed in supermarkets, where it may be purchased fresh or frozen. This recipe was tested with this product and is based on two 12-ounce packages containing 4 small loaves (without seeds) each.

2. Sprinkle half the slices with parsley and thyme and the other half with sesame seeds.

3. Toast under broiler about 1 to 1½ minutes, or until edges are almost black and bread is lightly toasted. Watch carefully; the slices burn easily. Yield: 32 slices.

> PRESENTATION: Serve hot on a wooden platter or in a basket. These are best served immediately, as they toughen on standing. For buffets wait until guests have served themselves the main dish, then toast and pass. Seconds may be kept hot in a turned-off oven with the door left open.

Note: You will have to do these in several batches as most broiler pans will accommodate only 2 rounds, split and cut, at one time. A helper in the kitchen will ease the process.

To prepare in advance: Complete step 1, or complete all steps (see *Note* below). Stack buttered sides together and store in a tightly closed plastic bag, pressing out as much air as possible. Try to do this as late as possible as the bread dries out quickly when cut, especially if not very fresh. (Frozen *pita* is often dry if kept in storage more than a few months.)

Note: I prefer to serve the *pita* when only lightly toasted as in the above recipe, but for convenience it may be first broiled for color, then placed in a 250° oven until the bread is *completely* dried. It will be crunchy all the way through and similar to melba toast. Do any time, cool and store at room temperature, but re-heat on a baking sheet when ready to serve. Second-best, but still delicious!

Cheesecake with Pineapple Glaze

Most cheesecakes are delicious; this one is superb.
Must be prepared in advance.

Crumb Crust (recipe below)
1   pound (two 8-ounce packages) cream cheese, soft-
      ened at room temperature
3   eggs, separated (at room temperature)
¾   cup sugar
2   tablespoons flour
1   can (5 ½ ounces) evaporated milk (⅔ cup)
1   teaspoon vanilla extract
½   teaspoon salt
1   jar (12 ounces) pineapple preserves (1 cup)

1. Prepare Crumb Crust as directed.
2. Cream cheese until fluffy with an electric beater. Beat in
egg yolks, one at a time. Gradually beat in ½ cup of sugar and
the flour. Stir in milk and vanilla.
3. Beat egg whites until foamy (using an electric beater), then
add salt and beat until soft peaks form. Gradually beat in the
remaining ¼ cup sugar, beating until very stiff and glossy, about
5 minutes. Fold into cheese mixture.
4. Spread a generous ¼ cup preserves over the Crumb Crust
(not on sides). Pour filling on top; level.
5. Bake in a preheated 325° oven for 45 to 50 minutes, or until
set.
6. Cool on a rack at room temperature, away from drafts.
Sprinkle reserved crumbs (see Crumb Crust recipe) around
edge and spoon the remaining ¾ cup pineapple preserves in the
center. Chill. May be made a day or two in advance.

PRESENTATION: Remove rim from bottom of
pan and place cheesecake (in its pan) on a serving platter. Cut in wedges to serve.

CRUMB CRUST

1 ½   cups vanilla wafer crumbs
4   tablespoons butter, melted (½ stick)
1   tablespoon lemon juice
1   tablespoon sugar

1. Mix crumbs, butter, lemon juice and sugar with a fork until crumbly. Remove ⅓ cup and reserve for garnish, then press *half* the remainder firmly on bottom of a 9-inch springform pan (sides removed).

2. Bake in a preheated 325° oven for 5 minutes; cool on a rack.

3. Put rim around bottom of pan and butter the inside. Press the remaining half of the crumb mixture about half way up the sides.

MENU
BUFFET

FIRST COURSE: *Fresh Clam Coquilles*

MAIN COURSE: *Veal Parmigiana*
· *Sautéed Zucchini Strips*
· *Hearts of Escarole with Italian Dressing*
· *Frozen Garlic Bread*

DESSERT: *Zuppa Inglese*
Espresso

· Quick and Easy Recipe

Fresh Clam Coquilles

Two dozen cherrystone clams are the beginning—and end—of this robust hot hors d'oeuvre. The clams are first steamed, then removed from the shells and combined with fresh shrimp, commercial bread stuffing, parsley, onion and garlic. The clam shells are retained for the baking and serving of the seafood mélange. *May be partially prepared in advance.*

24 cherrystone clams, cleaned (method below)
1 cup dry white wine
½ pound butter (1 cup)
¾ cup finely chopped onions
4 cloves garlic, put through a press
¾ cup minced parsley
1 pound raw shrimp, shelled and deveined and cut the size of peas
2½ cups commercial bread stuffing mix (Pepperidge Farm brand preferred)
Salt to taste (if necessary)

GARNISH:
Chopped parsley

1. Place cleaned clams in a large saucepan (preferably enamel).* Add the wine, cover, bring to a boil, lower heat and steam gently until open. These hard-shelled clams will take 10 to 15 minutes. Remove and cool. Strain broth through a tea towel wrung out in cold water to eliminate any grains of sand; reserve.

2. Discard any clams that did not open. Separate shells and reserve at least 32 half shells, cutting away and discarding the tough connecting muscle. Cut clams into small pieces, about the size of a small pea (there should be 1 cup).

3. Melt the butter in a large skillet. Add the chopped onions and garlic; sauté until translucent. Add the parsley, stuffing mix and cut-up shrimp. Stir once with a fork, then sprinkle the mixture with about 1 cup of the clam broth; sauté, stirring until the shrimp turn pink, about 2 or 3 minutes, and mixture begins to stick to the pan. Add a little more clam broth if mixture seems too dry. Stir in reserved chopped clams and remove from heat. Do not cook further. Salt to taste if necessary.

4. Spoon into the reserved clam shells. (This amount should fill 32 generously, but possibly more, depending on the size of the clams.) Arrange in a shallow baking pan.

5. Bake in a preheated 400° oven for 10 minutes, or until lightly browned. Yield: 32 or more coquilles.

PRESENTATION: Sprinkle with chopped parsley. Arrange on serving trays, cool slightly and pass to guests as a hot hors d'oeuvre, or arrange 2 to a plate and serve as a first course. Either way you will need cocktail forks. Pass the remaining coquilles for seconds.

To prepare in advance: Complete steps 1 through 4, up to baking. Cool. Cover with plastic wrap and refrigerate. Bake 5 minutes longer.

* If an aluminum saucepan is used the broth will be an unappetizing gray; but this will not be apparent in the finished coquilles.

To clean clams: Scrub shells clean under cold running water (a plastic pot scrubber is excellent). Discard any that will not close. Then soak in a bowl of fresh water for 1 hour, changing the water 2 or 3 times if necessary as the clams pump and purge themselves of any sand. Drain and store in the refrigerator until ready to steam open.

Veal Parmigiana

This recipe is very good made with supermarket mozzarella and Parmesan cheese, but if you can locate an Italian store in which to buy these ingredients, the casserole will be a degree better and more authentic. It may be frozen before baking.

May be partially prepared in advance.

3	pounds veal cutlets, sliced ¼ inch thick
3	eggs, slightly beaten
1½	teaspoons salt
½	teaspoon freshly ground pepper
	Fine dry bread crumbs (about 2 cups)
	Olive oil (about 1 cup)
6	cans (8-ounce size) tomato sauce
1	clove garlic, put through a press
1½	teaspoons dry basil
1	teaspoon Worcestershire sauce
½	teaspoon salt
2	tablespoons butter
½	cup freshly grated Parmesan cheese (method below)
1½	pounds mozzarella cheese, thinly sliced

GARNISH:
Paprika
Sprigs of parsley

1. Pound veal between 2 sheets of waxed paper to break down tissue and make a little thinner. Remove all fat and connecting

tissue. Unless very small, cut into 3-by-4-inch pieces. Pound again.

2. Bread the veal by first dipping into the eggs mixed with the salt and pepper, then into the bread crumbs to coat completely.

3. Slowly heat a large skillet; when very hot add a little of the olive oil. (Heating the pan, then adding the oil, will prevent the breading from sticking to pan when browning.) Add a few pieces of veal and lightly brown on both sides; remove to a shallow casserole, overlapping slightly. (You will no doubt need 2 casseroles for this amount.) Repeat with remaining veal, adding more oil as necessary.

4. Meanwhile, combine tomato sauce, garlic, basil, Worcestershire sauce and salt in a 2-quart saucepan. Bring to a boil, then simmer uncovered for 10 minutes. Remove from heat and stir in butter. When melted, pour over the browned veal in the casseroles (it will not cover completely). Sprinkle with the Parmesan cheese. Cover with aluminum foil.

5. Bake in a preheated 350° oven for 25 to 30 minutes. Then remove foil and top with mozzarella cheese. Return to oven, uncovered, and bake until cheese is melted, about 10 minutes.

PRESENTATION: Serve hot directly from casseroles, garnished with a dusting of paprika and a few sprigs of parsley. The mozzarella is stringy so 2 serving spoons will be needed.

To prepare in advance: Complete steps 1 through 4, up to baking, a day in advance if desired. Cover with plastic wrap, then foil. Refrigerate or freeze, but bring to room temperature before baking for accurate timing. (Remove plastic wrap.)

To grate Parmesan in a blender: Cut cheese in small chunks and blend a few at a time with blender set at "high," until finely grated.

Sautéed Zucchini Strips

Zucchini is a long, green Italian squash. It makes a colorful vegetable dish because it is not necessary to peel the thin skin. *May be partially prepared in advance.*

> 3 pounds zucchini (preferably small size)
> ½ cup olive oil
> 3 tablespoons butter
> Salt to taste

1. Scrub zucchini well to remove the sand but do not peel. Cut off ends. Then cut in quarters, once across and once lengthwise; then cut lengthwise in ¼-inch strips. (To do this easily, cut across, then stand on end and slice down in strips; reform and cut through once.)

2. Heat 2 large skillets over medium-high heat. Divide the butter and olive oil between the skillets. When the foam from the butter subsides, add the zucchini to the 2 skillets. First, turn over with a spatula to coat; then sauté over medium-high heat, turning occasionally, until cooked through but still tender-crisp, about 5 minutes. Some of the strips will have browned lightly; the rest should be golden yellow. (Remember, zucchini is delicious raw; it is better to undercook than to overcook.) Season lightly with salt.

PRESENTATION: Serve immediately on a heated serving platter, leaving the juices in the skillets.

To prepare in advance: Complete step 1 any time. The zucchini will not turn brown on standing, nor does it need to be salted to draw the juices. Cover with damp paper toweling and refrigerate. It is not necessary to bring to room temperature before sautéing.

Hearts of Escarole with Italian Dressing

Escarole is in the endive family. It has broad leaves with a somewhat bitter flavor and tender hearts with less bite. Only escarole with yellow, blanched hearts should be used in this recipe. The small addition of sugar in the dressing neutralizes the bitterness.

May be partially prepared in advance.

> Escarole (enough of the light green and yellow
>   hearts to make 4 quarts coarsely torn greens)
> ⅔ cup olive oil
> ¼ cup cider vinegar
> 2 tablespoons lemon juice
> 1 teaspoon salt
> 1 teaspoon sugar
> ½ teaspoon oregano
> ½ teaspoon dried, crushed hot Italian peppers
> 1 clove garlic, crushed with the flat of a knife

1. Wash the escarole in a sink filled with cold water. Discard core and any bruised leaves. Use the hearts only. (Save the outside leaves for mixed salads. These are tough and bitter, and need to be combined with sweeter, more tender greens.) Drain, then roll up in one layer in a terry-cloth towel, turning ends under. Refrigerate in the towel, which will absorb any remaining water. Store in the refrigerator at least 1 hour to crisp.

2. To make the dressing, measure the oil, vinegar, lemon juice, salt, sugar, oregano, dried hot peppers and crushed garlic clove into a screw-top jar. Cover and shake to blend seasonings. Set aside at least 1 hour to meld the flavors. Remove garlic clove before using.

3. When ready to serve, tear escarole into large bite-size pieces. Place in a salad bowl large enough to toss the greens easily. Shake the dressing and dribble it over the greens. Toss gently but thoroughly so escarole is well coated but not wilted.

PRESENTATION: Serve immediately directly from salad bowl.

To prepare in advance: Complete steps 1 and 2, up to tossing the salad. If desired, wash greens 1 or 2 days in advance and store in the towel in the refrigerator. Tear the day of serving. Dressing may be made a week in advance, but remove garlic clove after 24 hours.

Frozen Garlic Bread

There's no reason why garlic bread cannot be prepared well in advance and frozen. It is baked here without thawing first.
Must be prepared in advance.

    ½ pound butter (1 cup)
    8 cloves garlic, crushed with the flat of a knife
    2 long loaves (1 pound each) French bread

1. Melt the butter in a 2-quart saucepan over low heat; add the garlic cloves and sauté until golden. Remove from heat; discard the garlic.
2. Put each loaf of bread on a separate sheet of aluminum foil. Cut in 1½-inch diagonal slices, almost to the bottom. Spread slices apart and brush garlic butter generously between the slices. Press back into shape and brush crusts. Wrap foil tightly around the bread with the opening at the top, and freeze.
3. To heat, do not thaw. Open foil and bake in a preheated 350° oven for about 15 minutes, or until heated through and crust is crisp.

PRESENTATION: Serve hot in long French bread basket or on a board, letting guests pull off the slices.

Zuppa Inglese

Zuppa Inglese (or English soup) is an Italian dessert, so named perhaps because of its similarity to England's trifle. Its versions are innumerable, but none certainly more attractive or luscious than this one. Here the traditional layers of sponge cake are spread with custard, dotted with citron, currants and bitter chocolate and made heady with rum and crème de cacao. It is chilled overnight, or longer, so the filling seeps into the dry cake. And as a final glory, it is frosted with Italian unbaked meringue.
Must be prepared in advance.

      Custard Sauce (recipe below)
⅓ cup currants
⅓ cup light rum
 2 layers (9 to 10 inches each, at least 1½ inches high) sponge cake, from the bakery*
 2 tablespoons sliced citron
 1 square (1 ounce) unsweetened chocolate, shaved with a vegetable peeler
 5 tablespoons crème de cacao
      Italian Meringue (recipe below)

1. Prepare Custard Sauce and chill.
2. Soak currants in rum for 15 minutes. Reserve rum.
3. Split cake layers horizontally into 3 layers each, to make 6 in all. (This is easier if cake is chilled.) Place 1 layer, crust side down, in the bottom of a 9- to 10-inch springform pan with sides attached (for convenience in storing), or place directly on a cake plate.
4. Sprinkle the cake layer with a few of the soaked currants, a few slivers of citron and a little of the shaved chocolate; dribble about 1 tablespoon rum and 1 tablespoon crème de cacao over the top. Dribble about ½ cup of the custard over the top. Add

---

* Most bakeries sell unfrosted sponge layers; however, it may be necessary to order in advance.

another cake layer and repeat process, ending with a layer on top with crust side up. Leave top plain. Cover with plastic wrap and refrigerate at least 24 hours; it keeps well up to 1 week.

5. The day of serving (no more than 6 hours), remove rim from springform, prepare Italian Meringue and frost the cake. Set in a cool place, but do not refrigerate. The meringue will begin to dissolve when refrigerated, but because of the custard, the dessert must be kept somewhat cool.

PRESENTATION: Place frosted Zuppa Inglese on a cake platter (if springform pan was used). Cut in thick wedges with a cake server. (Wet server for easier cutting through meringue.)

To prepare in advance: Complete steps 1 through 4, up to frosting with Italian Meringue, which must be made and used the day of serving.

CUSTARD SAUCE

5 egg yolks
⅔ cup sugar
2½ tablespoons cornstarch
¼ teaspoon salt
2½ cups milk, heated until hot
1 teaspoon vanilla extract

1. Mix the egg yolks, sugar, cornstarch and salt in a heavy 2-quart saucepan; do not beat.

2. Slowly pour in the hot milk, stirring constantly with a rubber spatula. Set the saucepan over direct, medium heat; stir slowly until the mixture begins to thicken, then turn heat to low and stir more rapidly until it thickens further and coats a spoon with a thin, creamy layer. (Do not boil, or the sauce will curdle.)

Note: At first the mixture will foam; then, as it gradually gets hotter, the bubbles will subside, and just before it thickens a stream of vapor will rise. The gentle heat is necessary at this point or the eggs will overcook and curdle instead of gradually turning into a smooth, velvety sauce.

3. Remove from the heat and stir rapidly to bring the temperature down slightly; then stir in the vanilla. Set pan in a bowl of ice water, and stir until cool. Pour into a refrigerator container and chill.

ITALIAN MERINGUE

> ¾ cup white corn syrup
> 2 egg whites (¼ cup)
> ⅛ teaspoon salt
> 1 teaspoon vanilla extract

1. In a small saucepan, heat the corn syrup until bubbles appear around the edge.

2. Beat the egg whites with an electric beater until foamy; add salt and beat until stiff but not dry.

3. Slowly pour the hot corn syrup over the beaten egg whites, continuing to beat until meringue is fluffy and hangs in peaks from the beater. Fold in the vanilla.

Menus and Recipes for Sixteen

MENU
BUFFET

FIRST COURSE: *Colorful Canapés*
· *Turkish Almonds*

MAIN COURSE: *Chicken Divan*
· *Honeydew Melon and Green Grape Platter*
· *Pre-buttered Pan Rolls with Summer Savory*

DESSERT: *Meringues with Berries*
Coffee

· Quick and Easy Recipe

Colorful Canapés

You may never put a more inviting array of canapés before your guests than these made of rolled anchovies, shrimp, caviar and ham on rounds of white bread. Each is made colorful with a leaflet of parsley and a tiny wedge of cherry tomato. Like all fresh canapés, they must be prepared the day they are served.
May be prepared in advance.

2 loaves (1 pound each) sliced white bread (Pepperidge Farm type)
½ cup butter, softened (¼ pound)
4 hard-cooked egg yolks (method below)
⅛ teaspoon salt
2 packages (3-ounce size) cream cheese, softened
Black caviar
Boiled Virginia ham, finely chopped
Rolled anchovies stuffed with capers, drained well
Tiny canned shrimp (Pacific Pearl is a good brand), drained

GARNISH:
Small cherry tomatoes, cut in thin wedges
Leaflets of parsley

1. Cut bread into small rounds with a cutter, using one small enough to obtain 3 rounds from each bread slice. There should be no crusts on the rounds. Out of the 2 loaves you should have about 90 rounds.

2. As you cut the bread, place the rounds on their sides in rows in a square cake pan. When all are cut, loosely cover with a sheet of waxed paper and cover entire pan with a dampened tea towel.

Note: Whirl bread crusts in a blender for later use as fresh bread crumbs. Store in a screw-top jar in the freezer; use directly from the jar while still frozen; they thaw immediately.

3. Whip butter with a fork until creamy. Quarter and press the hard-cooked egg yolks through a sieve directly into the whipped butter; blend. Season with salt. Spread smoothly on some of the bread rounds, and top each with a dab of caviar *or* some chopped boiled ham.

4. Whip the cream cheese with a few drops of water with a fork until fluffy. Spread smoothly on remainder of the bread rounds, and top with either a rolled anchovy *or* 3 tiny shrimp and a few grains of caviar.

5. Garnish each canapé with a thin wedge of cherry tomato and a tiny leaflet (not a sprig) of parsley.

6. Arrange 1 layer deep in shallow containers (cake pans, plastic refrigerator storage boxes or the like). Put waxed paper loosely on top and cover with a dampened tea towel, or a double thickness of paper toweling wrung out in water. Refrigerate up to 6 hours, if desired; longer than that, the tomatoes and parsley tend to dry out. Remove from the refrigerator 10 to 20 minutes before serving to allow the butter-egg and cream cheese spreads to soften slightly. Keep covered for freshness. Yield: 90 canapés.

PRESENTATION: Arrange on serving trays. Small ones are best; they can be replenished easily. Pass 1 or 2 trays at a time to keep from drying out.

To prepare in advance: Complete all steps and refrigerate, up to 6 hours. The bread rounds may be cut and stored 2 days in the refrigerator if preferred. Freezing tends to dry them out.

To hard-cook egg yolks: Carefully separate yolks from whites, without breaking yolks. (This is easier if the eggs are cold.) One by one place in a spoon and lower into simmering water; simmer 10 minutes, or until cooked through. (The egg whites may be stored in a screw-top jar in the refrigerator for a week or so, or they may be frozen.)

Turkish Almonds

Turkish almonds are crisp, cool and unique. In Turkey, vendors sell these almonds piled in a pyramid on top of a huge block of ice. They are shelled, but unblanched—still in the raw state. The nuts are peeled from their skins one by one before eating. For ease, I suggest serving them blanched and from a bowl set in crushed ice. The rosewater gives a pleasant and characteristic flavor but may be omitted—salt lightly instead.

Must be prepared in advance.

> ½ pound shelled, unblanched almonds
> Cold water
> Rosewater*
>
> SERVING CONTAINER:
> A bowl set in a platter of crushed ice

1. To blanch, pour boiling water (to cover) over the almonds. Let stand 3 minutes; drain in a colander. While warm, slip off skins by pinching between fingers.
2. Put in a bowl, cover with cold water and refrigerate for 3 or 4 hours to crisp, or leave overnight if desired. Yield: 1½ cups.

* Rosewater is a scented flavoring made from oil of fresh roses and water. It is highly regarded in the Middle Eastern countries, where it is used primarily in beverages and desserts. Rosewater is available in stores specializing in Greek and Turkish foods. Sometimes it is sold in drugstores.

PRESENTATION: Fill a small chilled serving platter or shallow bowl with crushed ice and nestle a small
bowl in the center. Drain the almonds and sprinkle with
the rosewater to scent lightly. Pour into the small bowl
set in the ice and serve immediately.

To prepare in advance: Complete all steps and part of Presentation, up to putting the nuts in the bowl. Keep platter filled with
ice in the freezer.

Chicken Divan

Chicken Divan originated in the 1920's in a New York restaurant called Divan Parisien, back when broccoli was virtually
unknown to all except the Italians. Versions have multiplied since
then. This is one variation not containing hollandaise, which the
original required. It is, however, excellent.
May be partially prepared in advance.

    9 whole chicken breasts (about 8 pounds)
    3 ribs of celery, including leaves, cut in half
    1 large onion, cut in quarters
    1 tablespoon salt
   12 whole peppercorns
    3 quarts cold water
   3¼ cups chicken broth (reserved from cooking breasts)
   1½ cups dry sherry
    ¾ cup butter (1½ sticks)
    ¾ cup flour
    2 cups milk
    1 cup heavy cream
    1 tablespoon salt
    4 egg yolks, slightly beaten
   1½ cups freshly grated Parmesan cheese (see Index II)
    6 pounds fresh broccoli (3 to 4 bunches), blanched
        and refreshed (see Index II)

1. Put the chicken breasts in a large kettle with celery ribs, onion, salt, peppercorns and cold water. Bring to a boil, skim, then reduce heat to simmer and cook uncovered 30 to 40 minutes, or until tender. Remove from the heat. Strain broth, discarding seasonings; skim off fat and use for other purpose. Reserve 3¼ cups broth.

2. When the chicken is cool enough to handle, remove the skin and discard. Pull the meat from the bones in ⅛- to ¼-inch-thick slices. Place on a platter and sprinkle ½ cup of the sherry over the pieces to moisten. Set aside to marinate while making the sauce.

3. Melt the butter in a 4-quart, heavy saucepan. Add the flour and cook and stir 5 minutes over low heat, but do not brown.

4. Combine the milk, cream, and chicken broth in a separate saucepan; heat until bubbles appear around the edge. Gradually add to butter-and-flour mixture, stirring constantly, and cook until thickened and smooth. Add the 1 tablespoon salt and remove from heat. Dribble about 1 cup of the sauce into the slightly beaten egg yolks, stirring constantly. Add to remaining sauce. Cook 2 to 3 minutes, stirring. The sauce must not boil or the eggs will curdle. It should be smooth and only slightly thickened.

Remove from heat and stir in half the Parmesan cheese (¾ cup). After 5 minutes, stir in the remaining 1 cup dry sherry. Set aside.

5. Grease 2 or 3 large shallow casseroles (total capacity about 8 quarts). Arrange sliced, cooked broccoli over the bottom. Place the chicken on the broccoli, then pour the warm sauce over all, but leave a little broccoli showing around the edge. Sprinkle with remaining ¾ cup grated Parmesan cheese.

6. Bake uncovered in a preheated 350° oven for 20 to 30 minutes, or until top is delicately golden and the chicken and broccoli are piping hot. If baking on 2 levels, switch casseroles halfway through to brown evenly.

PRESENTATION: Serve hot from casseroles. No garnish is necessary.

To prepare in advance: Prepare the broccoli and complete steps 1 through part of 5, up to adding the sauce. Cover and refrigerate the chicken and broccoli, but bring to room temperature before baking. Store the sauce separately, floating a film of milk over the top to keep a skin from forming. Reheat slowly when ready to use.

Honeydew Melon and Green Grape Platter

Crescents of juicy green melon and crisp green grapes are sweetened in an unusual way with orange juice concentrate straight from the can. The coolness of the pale greens is enhanced with a garnish of fresh mint.
May be partially prepared in advance.

2 or 3 honeydew melons, chilled
3 cups green grapes, halved and seeded (or use seedless), chilled
1 can (6 ounces) frozen orange-juice concentrate, thawed but undiluted

GARNISH:
Fresh mint sprigs or watercress

1. Slice the melons in half lengthwise; remove seeds, then peel and cut across in thin slices (about ⅜ inch thick). Arrange spoke fashion, overlapping slightly, on a large platter.
2. Put seeded and halved grapes in the center.
3. Brush melon slices and grapes generously with the thawed orange-juice concentrate.

PRESENTATION: Serve chilled, the platter garnished with mint sprigs. Include a flat server and spoon for serving.

To prepare in advance: Complete steps 1 and 2, up to brushing with the orange juice. Cover with plastic wrap and chill. (The concentrate will draw the juices from the fruit if added too far in advance.)

Pre-buttered Pan Rolls with Summer Savory

Packaged yeast rolls are used in this recipe, but the pre-buttering and herbs give them a decided lift. The combination melts into the warm bread, making the rolls seem homemade.
May be prepared in advance.

   3 packages purchased pan rolls (12 tiny rolls each)*
  ¾ cup butter, softened (1½ sticks)
1½ teaspoons summer savory, crushed

1. Remove rolls from package but leave in foil pan; pull slightly apart. Spread with softened butter and sprinkle with summer savory. Return to package and let stand at room temperature until ready to serve.
2. Reheat in foil pans, at any temperature (between 300° and 400°), until very hot. Yield: 36 rolls.

> PRESENTATION: Remove from pans in large rounds and place each on a warm serving plate. Let guests break them apart.

Meringues with Berries

These individual desserts are beautiful. Crisp meringues are filled with nothing more than whipped cream and perfect red strawberries dusted with confectioners' sugar. The combination of flavors and the contrast of textures are simple but outstanding. The meringue is easy, provided that you own an electric beater

---

* Pepperidge Farm Old Fashioned Rolls (7-ounce package) were used in testing this recipe.

and follow directions exactly. They can be made weeks in advance if desired and the filling can be added up to 2 hours before serving.

May be prepared in advance.

6　egg whites, at room temperature (¾ cup)
2　cups sugar (superfine is best)
1½　teaspoons lemon juice

GARNISHES:
Stiffly whipped cream (½ pint)
2 or 3 fresh strawberries for each meringue
Curaçao
Confectioners' sugar

1. Beat the egg whites in a large mixing bowl until they are stiff and hold a point, but are not dry. (An electric beater is necessary.) Gradually beat in 1 cup of sugar (if it is not added slowly enough the meringues will be granular). Gradually add remaining 1 cup sugar alternately with the lemon juice, beating until the sugar is completely dissolved (test with fingers). The meringue should be stiff and glossy.

2. Cut 2 pieces of heavy brown paper to fit 2 large baking sheets. Mark eight 3-inch circles on each paper 1½ inches apart. Drop a generous spoonful of meringue into the center of each. Using a teaspoon spread to edges of circles, hollowing out the center of each meringue to form a cavity.

3. Bake in a preheated 225° oven for 1 hour to 1 hour and 20 minutes, or until dried and crisp. (They should be white, not cream-colored.) Remove and cool on paper. Peel off paper, using a spatula to loosen if necessary. (The variation in time is due to variation in oven temperatures at this low range, and weather.)

4. Store in a loosely covered container. These keep for weeks. Yield: 16 meringues.

Note: Meringues should be made on a dry day for proper beating and baking.

5. Rinse strawberries quickly, hull and dry on paper toweling. One or 2 hours before filling meringues, sprinkle berries with 1

or 2 tablespoons curaçao. (This will sweeten the berries slightly and give a dewy look without drawing the juices.)

> PRESENTATION: Fill shells with whipped cream and put 3 small or 2 large strawberries, point up, in each meringue. Garnish tops with a pinch of confectioners' sugar.

To prepare in advance: Make meringues any time, completing steps 1 through 4. Up to 2 hours before serving, fill and garnish; refrigerate. Dust with confectioners' sugar just before serving. The meringues should be tender but crisp. If filled too far in advance they will soften.

MENU
BUFFET

FIRST COURSE: *Four Canapé Pies*

MAIN COURSE: *Veal Scaloppine Bolognese*
Spinach with Ricotta
Green Salad with Italian Parsley and
Artichoke Hearts
Grissini, Italian Bread Sticks

DESSERT: *Chocolate Marquise in Sauce Anglaise*
Espresso

Four Canapé Pies

Crusty rounds of black bread cut from a large round loaf are the basis here for 4 mosaic compositions. The coarse, moist bread in combination with a smooth egg spread, smoky sardines and salty caviar provide a tasty and attractive canapé, which can be picked up and eaten out of hand.

Should be prepared in advance.

- 1 round loaf of sour rye or pumpernickel (7 inches in diameter)
- 6 hard-cooked eggs
- 3 tablespoons mayonnaise (about)
- ½ teaspoon dry mustard (or to taste)
- ½ teaspoon garlic salt (or to taste)
- 64 brisling sardines* (in olive oil), drained on paper toweling

* Brisling sardines come from Norway. They are slightly smoked, small and silver-colored. They are available at most supermarkets. Purchase cans that indicate "very small" or "packed in two layers," as the size varies somewhat. You will need 3 3¾-ounce cans for the required number.

1 jar (4 ounces) black caviar (dyed white lumpfish
     will do)
8 cherry tomatoes, cut in quarters

GARNISH:
Chopped scallions
Chopped parsley

1. Slice loaf of bread horizontally into four ⅓-inch-thick
rounds, discarding top and bottom crusts. Leave outer crust on
rounds.

2. Cut hard-cooked eggs in quarters and press through a sieve
into a small bowl. Stir in enough mayonnaise to moisten for
spreading. Season with mustard and garlic salt. Spread on tops
of bread rounds to edges.

3. Slice each round into 8 pie-shaped wedges, then re-form
on 4 small serving plates.

4. On each wedge (at the outer edge), arrange 2 sardines, tails
toward the center. Between each two, at the outer edge, put a dab
of mayonnaise, and anchor a wedge of tomato on each, cut side
up. In the center of each re-formed round, mark a 2-inch circle
with a cookie cutter or glass. Spread with caviar.

5. Sprinkle each entire round with chopped scallions and
chopped parsley. Cover with plastic wrap and refrigerate several
hours to mellow. About an hour before serving, remove from refrigerator, but leave plastic wrap on until ready to serve.

PRESENTATION: Pass to guests on the serving
plates. These canapés are firm enough to be eaten out
of hand. There are 32 wedges, allowing 2 per person.

Veal Scaloppine Bolognese

This is one of those entrees which, when well done, can create
a loyal following for an Italian restaurant. However, it is also a
specialty that may be prepared with equal success at home. Strips

of veal are simmered with mushrooms in a rich wine sauce until the liquid is reduced to a glaze. Then a generous amount of Parmesan cheese is melted in for character.

May be partially prepared in advance.

       4 pounds veal cutlets, sliced ¼ inch thick
    1¾ cups flour
       4 teaspoons salt
       ½ teaspoon freshly ground pepper
      12 tablespoons butter, clarified (1½ sticks) (see Index II)
       1 pound fresh mushrooms, wiped and thinly sliced
       ¾ cup olive oil (about)
       3 cups finely chopped onion (3 medium onions)
       1 cup finely chopped celery
       ¼ cup minced parsley
       8 cloves garlic, minced
       2 cups rich chicken broth
       1 cup dry white wine or vermouth
       1 cup dry sherry (good quality)
       ¾ cup freshly grated Parmesan cheese*

GARNISH:
       3 lemons, thinly sliced
       1 cup minced parsley

1. Veal should be sliced ¼ inch thick, as for the usual scaloppine, then pounded between 2 sheets of waxed paper to break down the tissues and make a little thinner. Remove all fat and connecting tissue. Cut into bite-size strips; dry on paper toweling. Mix flour, salt and pepper together and dredge meat strips in this mixture. Shake off excess in a sieve.

2. Heat a large heavy skillet, then add 6 tablespoons of the clarified butter; when hot, toss in mushrooms. Sauté over medium-high heat until lightly browned, 4 to 5 minutes shaking the pan occasionally to cook evenly. (The mushrooms will absorb

---

* The quality of the cheese is important. Buy a whole piece of imported Parmesan and grate your own. (See Index II for grating in blender.) Or buy it freshly grated at an Italian specialty shop.

the butter at first, but will release it when cooked through.) Remove mushrooms and set aside.

3. Add a little of the remaining butter and a little of the olive oil to the same skillet. Add a layer of veal strips (do not crowd), and sauté over medium-high heat, browning lightly on both sides, about 1 minute to a side. Remove and set aside. Repeat process with remaining veal strips, adding more butter and oil as necessary.

Note: You will find it convenient to use 2 large skillets to sauté this amount of meat (and mushrooms) because you can sauté only about ¼ pound of meat at a time.

4. When all the meat is browned and removed, add the onions, celery, parsley and garlic. Sauté over medium heat until onions are golden. Stir in chicken broth, scraping up all browned bits sticking to the skillet; then simmer, uncovered, 15 minutes.

5. Stir in the white wine and sherry. Then add veal strips and simmer, uncovered, for 15 minutes. (The sauce should be rich-looking and greatly reduced, leaving not much more than a glaze on the meat.) Add the sautéed mushrooms the last 5 minutes to reheat. Just before removing from heat, stir in grated Parmesan cheese. It will melt at once.

PRESENTATION: Spoon onto a hot platter, sprinkle with chopped parsley and garnish edge with lemon slices.

To prepare in advance: Prepare steps 1 through part of 5, up to adding the mushrooms; cool. When ready to serve, add the mushrooms, bring to a boil, reduce heat and simmer 5 minutes. Stir in Parmesan cheese.

Spinach with Ricotta

This unusual vegetable dish is also called *gnocchi* or green ravioli. A mixture of chopped cooked spinach and ricotta cheese

is formed into balls or oval shapes, then basted with butter and chicken broth when heated for serving. Delicate and delicious.
May be partially prepared in advance.

> 8 packages (10-ounce size) frozen chopped spinach
> 1 pound ricotta cheese*
> 6 tablespoons grated Parmesan cheese
> 2 teaspoons salt
> 1 teaspoon freshly ground pepper
> ½ teaspoon freshly ground nutmeg
> ½ pound butter (1 cup)
> 2 cups chicken broth, boiled down rapidly to 1 cup

1. Let spinach stand at room temperature until almost thawed. Chop fine. (To do this easily, cut lengthwise, then across each block in ¼-inch slices.)

2. Cook spinach in water according to package directions, but without seasoning. Drain in a colander, pressing with a spoon to extract most of the liquid. When cool, squeeze by handfuls to extract remainder.

3. If ricotta seems extra moist, drain it in a colander. Then add to spinach along with Parmesan cheese, salt, pepper and nutmeg, using hands to blend well. Form into 2-inch balls or oval shapes. (If necessary, refrigerate first until firm enough to mold.) There should be about 48 balls or ovals.

4. Melt butter in 2 large skillets and arrange spinach balls in each in 1 layer, turning to coat well. Dribble the reduced chicken broth over the top.

5. Cook over low heat, basting the balls with the pan juices until thoroughly hot and ready to serve, about 10 to 15 minutes. (Do not allow them to brown.)

PRESENTATION: Arrange carefully in a heated serving dish, pouring pan juices over the top.

* Ricotta is a smooth white Italian cheese, available in most supermarkets. Small-curd cottage cheese may be substituted, but it must be well drained and pressed through a coarse wire sieve.

To prepare in advance: Complete steps 1 through 4, up to heating; this can be done even the day before. Cover and refrigerate.

Green Salad with Italian Parsley and Artichoke Hearts

This is a basic tossed salad with the addition of flavorful Italian parsley and marinated artichokes right out of a jar.
May be partially prepared in advance.

> Romaine, chicory and iceberg lettuce—enough mixed
>   greens to make 6 quarts coarsely torn leaves
> 1 small bunch of Italian parsley*
> 2 jars (4-ounce size) marinated artichoke hearts
> 1 cup plus 2 tablespoons oil (olive oil drained from
>   artichokes and salad oil)
> ⅓ cup red wine vinegar
> 1 teaspoon dry mustard
> 2 teaspoons salt (or to taste)

1. Wash romaine and chicory in a sink filled with water; drain briefly. Tear into large bite-size pieces, discarding cores and any brown edges. Roll up in 1 layer in a terry-cloth towel, turning ends under. Refrigerate in the towel. It will absorb any remaining moisture. Store in the refrigerator at least 1 hour to crisp.

2. Store the head of iceberg lettuce in the refrigerator until ready to toss greens, then discard outer leaves and remove core. Pull off lettuce in small chunks. It is not necessary to wash. (Iceberg lettuce torn too far in advance may "rust" on the edges.)

3. Wash Italian parsley; drain briefly. Pull off leaflets and discard stems, or use for soup stock. Dry leaflets on paper toweling. Roll up in dry paper toweling and refrigerate, or use immediately.

* Italian parsley has large, broad, flat leaves, and has more flavor than the curly variety. Once purchased, it can be kept fresh, up to 2 weeks, stored in this manner: Stand the bunch of parsley upright in water in a wide-mouth jar, enclose (container and all) in a plastic bag and refrigerate.

4. To make the dressing, drain off olive oil from artichoke hearts and add enough salad oil to equal 1 cup plus 2 tablespoons. Cut any extra-large artichokes in 2 and refrigerate.

5. Measure the oil, vinegar, dry mustard and salt into a 1-pint screw-top jar. Put on lid and shake to blend seasonings. Set aside until ready to use. Do not refrigerate.

6. Just before serving place chilled greens, iceberg lettuce, parsley and artichokes in 1 or 2 bowls, large enough for tossing easily. Shake the dressing, then dribble over the greens. Toss gently but thoroughly, so greens are well coated but not wilted. Some of the artichoke leaves should pull away; this is desirable. Taste and correct seasoning. Serve immediately.

PRESENTATION: Place salad bowl on table with salad servers, serving guests or letting them help themselves.

To prepare in advance: Complete steps 1 through 5, up to tossing the salad. If desired, wash greens, but not parsley (unless left on stems), 1 or 2 days ahead and store in the towel in the refrigerator, but do not tear them until the day of serving as they may lose their crispness and turn brown on the edges.

Grissini, Italian Bread Sticks

These are crusty Italian bread sticks with soft insides, almost like skinny loaves of bread. Like any yeast bread, they are time-consuming to make, but are fun to do and may be frozen well in advance. Once thawed, *grissini* should be reheated to crisp.

May be prepared in advance.

    1   package active dry yeast
    ⅛ teaspoon salt
    ½ teaspoon sugar
    ¼ cup lukewarm water

  2 tablespoons sugar
  2 teaspoons salt
  ¼ cup butter, softened
  1 ¾ cups hot water
  5 to 6 cups unsifted all-purpose flour (preferably un-
      bleached type)

GLAZE:
1 unbeaten egg white and 1 tablespoon cold water

GARNISH:
Sesame seeds
Coarse salt

ACCOMPANIMENT:
Whipped butter (purchased)

1. Add yeast, the ⅛ teaspoon salt and the ½ teaspoon sugar
to ¼ cup of lukewarm water. Stir; let stand until it foams, about
5 minutes.

2. Combine the 2 tablespoons sugar, the 2 teaspoons salt and
the butter in a large mixing bowl. Add hot water and stir to dissolve sugar and melt butter. Cool to lukewarm and add the yeast
mixture.

3. Gradually stir in 3 cups of the flour, beating with a wooden
spoon until smooth and elastic. Stir in 2 to 3 cups more flour to
make a soft dough that does not stick to the fingers.

4. Turn dough onto a lightly floured board and knead until
smooth and elastic, about 5 minutes.

5. Shape the dough into a ball and put it into a greased bowl;
turn so greased side of dough is up, then cover and let rise in a
warm place until doubled in bulk, about 1½ hours.

6. Punch dough down; cut in half and form each half into a
smooth ball.

7. Roll half the dough at a time on a floured board into a rec-
tangle 7 inches wide and 12 inches long. Cut across into 24 strips
about ½ inch wide. Roll strips on the floured board with palms
of the hands into pencil-like sticks, about 10 inches long. (It is not
necessary to have them perfect; when baked they will have an

attractive home-baked look.) Transfer to a greased baking sheet, spacing them an inch apart. Repeat with remaining dough. (You will need 4 large baking sheets for the 48 sticks.)

8. Cover with dry paper toweling and let rise in a warm place until double in bulk, about 30 minutes. (They should feel slightly puffed.)

9. Brush the tops with unbeaten egg white mixed with the cold water (beat with a fork just enough to blend). Sprinkle with sesame seeds and coarse salt.

10. Bake in a preheated 425° oven 13 to 15 minutes (2 sheets at a time), or until golden brown. Cool on racks. (They may be stacked; arrange so that the air can circulate among them.) Yield: 48 bread sticks.

Note: Serve same day; reheat to warm if desired. Or wrap and freeze. Thaw, wrapped, at room temperature and reheat to crisp the crust.

> PRESENTATION: Serve warm (best) or at room temperature. Stand upright in a deep container, or arrange in a basket. Provide whipped butter for spreading if desired.

Chocolate Marquise in Sauce Anglaise

The ultimate in rich desserts: a square of creamy chocolate floating in a pool of warm, soft custard.
May be prepared in advance.

6 squares (1 ounce each) unsweetened chocolate
¾ cup sweet butter, softened (1½ sticks)
¾ cup sifted confectioners' sugar
3 eggs, separated
½ teaspoon vanilla extract
⅛ teaspoon salt
Sauce Anglaise (recipe below)

1. Melt the chocolate in a small skillet over *very low* heat. Stir to melt evenly. Remove from heat, stir and set aside to cool slightly.

2. Cream the butter and the sugar together. Add egg yolks, one at a time, beating well to incorporate. Stir in the cooled, melted chocolate and the vanilla.

3. Beat the egg whites until foamy; add the salt and beat until stiff but not dry. Fold into the chocolate mixture.

4. Spread in a buttered 8- by 8-inch-square pan, swirling the top to make it attractive. Refrigerate, covered with plastic wrap, several hours or overnight before serving. Then cut into sixteen 2-inch squares.

PRESENTATION: Fill sherbet glasses ⅔ full (about ⅓ cup per serving) of warm Sauce Anglaise. Float a square of the cold chocolate in the center. Serve immediately.

Note: If the chocolate is very firm, let it stand in the custard a few minutes before serving; it should be fairly soft, so that it melts in the mouth.

To prepare in advance: Make Chocolate Marquise, steps 1 through 4, and refrigerate. Make Sauce Anglaise. Set pan in a bowl of ice water, and stir until cool. Cover and refrigerate. Reheat gently over hot water when ready to serve. It should be warm, not hot.

SAUCE ANGLAISE

         4 egg yolks
        ⅔ cup sugar
         5 teaspoons cornstarch
        ⅛ teaspoon salt (scant)
         4 cups milk, heated until hot
      1½ teaspoons vanilla extract

1. Mix the egg yolks, sugar, cornstarch and salt in a heavy 3-quart saucepan; do not beat.

2. Slowly pour in the hot milk, stirring constantly with a rubber spatula. Set the saucepan over direct, medium heat. Stir slowly until the mixture begins to thicken, then turn heat to low and stir more rapidly until sauce is thick enough to coat a spoon with a thin creamy layer.

Note: At first the mixture will foam, then as it gradually gets hotter the bubbles will subside and just before it thickens a stream of vapor will rise. The gentle heat is necessary at this point or the eggs will overcook and curdle instead of gradually turning into a smooth velvety sauce.

3. Remove from heat and stir rapidly to bring the temperature down slightly; then stir in the vanilla. Cover and allow the custard to cool until just warm.

MENU
BUFFET

FIRST COURSE: *Pâté de Foie Liégeois*
Party Rye
Unsalted Crackers
Onion Rounds with Parsley Edge

MAIN COURSE: *Chicken Fondue*
· *Sautéed Watercress*
Celériac Rémoulade
· *Sliced Tomatoes with Sieved Egg Garnish*

DESSERT: · *Crème de Menthe Torte*
Coffee

· Quick and Easy Recipe

Pâté de Foie Liégeois

This pâté is truly remarkable—2 parts chicken liver and 1 part butter, delicately seasoned with dry mustard, cloves and nutmeg. If you are a pâté enthusiast, enough said. The recipe comes from Liège in Belgium.
Must be prepared in advance.

2 pounds chicken livers
1 medium onion, cut in quarters
Boiling water
1 pound butter, softened (2 cups)
4 teaspoons dry mustard
½ teaspoon ground cloves (scant)
½ teaspoon freshly grated nutmeg

GARNISH:
1 hard-cooked egg yolk (see Index II)

Parsley sprigs
Ripe olives

ACCOMPANIMENT:
Thinly sliced party rye bread (2 loaves)
Unsalted crackers

1. Rinse livers. Put livers and onion in a saucepan and add boiling water to cover. Simmer gently until tender and barely done, about 10 minutes. Drain and dry livers on paper toweling; discard onion.

2. While warm, put livers in an electric blender, ⅓ at a time, and blend until smooth. (Or use a food grinder with fine blade. This method is best if livers are very soft and tender.) Cool while preparing butter mixture.

3. Beat butter with mustard, cloves and nutmeg until light and fluffy. Combine with cooled liver paste.

4. Pack firmly in an oiled 3-cup round, straight-sided mold. Cover with plastic wrap and chill well. (Keeps several days well sealed and refrigerated.)

5. Before serving, remove from refrigerator to allow pâté to soften just enough for spreading, 1 to 2 hours. Unmold while chilled by dipping mold quickly in hot water to loosen pâté. Run a knife around the edge to loosen completely; invert on a large serving platter. Smooth with knife if necessary.

PRESENTATION: Garnish the top with hard-cooked egg yolk put through a sieve directly over pâté. Put sprigs of parsley and ripe olives around the base. (To keep shiny, dry olives, dip in oil and roll excess off on paper toweling.) Surround with slices of party rye and crackers. Include a spreading knife.

Onion Rounds with Parsley Edge

The onion here provides a perfect complement to the pâté. These are small party sandwiches of thin slices of onion, spread with mayonnaise and seasoned with salt. Enclosed in 2 rounds of firm white bread, the completed sandwiches are rolled lightly in mayonnaise, then in chopped parsley for a decorative edge. *May be prepared in advance.*

> 1½ loaves (1-pound size) thin-sliced white bread
>   (Pepperidge Farm type)
> 1 large bunch parsley (curly variety), freshened
>   (method below)
> 4 small onions, peeled and very thinly sliced
>   Blender Mayonnaise (see Index II)
>   Salt

1. Cut bread into small rounds with a cutter, using one small enough to obtain 3 rounds from each bread slice. There should be no crusts. Out of the 1½ loaves you should have about 68 rounds.

2. As you cut the bread, place the rounds on edge in rows in a square cake pan. When all are cut, loosely cover with a sheet of waxed paper and cover entire pan with a dampened tea towel.

Note: Whirl bread crusts in a blender for later use as fresh bread crumbs. Store in a screw-top jar in the freezer; use directly from the jar while frozen; they thaw immediately.

3. Chop parsley, using only the leaflets; save the stalks for soup stock.

4. To assemble, put a handful of the chopped parsley on a plate; spread a thin coating of mayonnaise on another. Spread 1 side of a bread round thinly with mayonnaise from the jar, place an onion slice on top and sprinkle lightly with salt; spread another bread round with mayonnaise and place that side down on the onion to form a sandwich. (Be certain the onion slice is no larger than the bread rounds; remove a ring or two if it is.)

Note: If onions are very strong, soak slices in cold water for 1 hour.

5. Holding the rounds in your fingers like a wheel, run edges lightly through mayonnaise on the plate, and then through the parsley. Return to cake pan, flat side down. Repeat with re-

mainder, placing waxed paper between layers and on top. Cover with a damp tea towel and refrigerate until ready to serve. Yield: about 34 canapes.

> PRESENTATION: Arrange sandwiches, cut in half if preferred, on a serving tray and pass. Or arrange a few around the Pâté de Foie Liégeois and replenish when necessary.

To prepare in advance: Complete all steps, but no longer than a few hours in advance, as the mayonnaise tends to seep into the bread. However, the bread rounds may be cut and stored as directed 2 days in advance. The onions may be peeled and stored 1 or 2 days in the refrigerator.

To freshen parsley: Wash bunch; shake off excess water and blot on paper toweling, then wrap in crumpled, dry paper toweling and store in a plastic bag in the refrigerator until dry and crisp. (This may be done several days in advance.)

Chicken Fondue

This is a recipe that uses every part of a "boiled" chicken except the bone: the flesh, the giblets, the skin, the rendered chicken fat and the broth. It is perfect for the cook who likes to get something for virtually nothing. It is a tri-level casserole containing an herb bread stuffing, a layer of tender chicken and a creamy layer of sauce. The topping is almost pure essence of chicken: crisp ground skin combined with bread crumbs (from the crusts).

May be partially prepared in advance.

  2 4½- to 5-pound chickens (preferably fat hens)
  2 ribs of celery, cut in half
  1 onion, cut in quarters
  4 teaspoons salt
 16 whole peppercorns
  3 quarts cold water

2 loaves (1-pound size) white bread (Pepperidge
     Farm type)
½ cup butter (1 stick)
½ cup chicken fat (reserved from broth)
2 cups finely chopped onions
2 cups finely chopped celery
1 tablespoon salt
1½ teaspoons freshly ground pepper
2 teaspoons dried sage
2 teaspoons poultry seasoning
½ cup chicken broth (reserved)
6 cups chicken broth (reserved)
1½ cups milk
1¼ cups chicken fat (reserved from broth) (or part
     butter)
1¼ cups unsifted all-purpose flour
1 tablespoon salt
6 eggs, beaten until frothy

GARNISH:
Chopped parsley

1. Cut up chickens to fit conveniently in a large kettle. Add
giblets, celery ribs, onion, the 4 teaspoons salt, peppercorns and
cold water. Bring to a boil, skim, then turn heat down, and simmer, covered, 2½ to 3 hours, or until the meat begins to pull
away from the bones. Remove from heat. Strain broth, discarding
seasonings, and skim off fat. Reserve fat, broth and giblets.

2. When chicken is cool enough to handle, remove the skin
and reserve. Pull the meat from the bones into about ¼-inch-
thick pieces; set aside (there should be at least 2 quarts loosely
packed meat).

3. Spread skin in a baking pan and bake in the highest position
in a preheated 400° oven for 15 minutes or until most of the skin
is crisp. Pour off fat. Cool.

4. To make the stuffing, thinly trim the crusts from the bread
and reserve. Cut remainder in ½-inch cubes. Place in a large
bowl and set aside.

5. Melt the ½ cup butter with the ½ cup chicken fat in a large skillet. Add the chopped onions and chopped celery; sauté until tender, about 5 to 10 minutes, but do not brown. Add to bread cubes along with the 1 tablespoon salt, the pepper, sage and poultry seasoning. Use a fork to toss and distribute evenly. Dribble ½ cup chicken broth over the top and toss again. Set aside.

6. To make the sauce heat the 6 cups chicken broth and the milk until bubbles appear around the edge. Pour 1¼ cups of the reserved chicken fat into a 4-quart heavy saucepan. Add the flour, cook and stir 5 minutes over low heat, but do not brown. Gradually add the hot milk and chicken broth, stirring constantly, until thickened and smooth; remove from heat and add salt. Dribble about 3 cups of the sauce into the beaten eggs, stirring constantly. Add to remaining sauce. Cook 2 to 3 minutes longer, stirring constantly. Cool slightly.

7. Using a blender, chop enough reserved bread crusts to make 1½ cups crumbs. Grind chicken skin (crisp part only) in a meat grinder, using the coarse blade. Combine with crumbs; reserve for topping. Grind giblets, set aside.

8. Grease a large casserole or 2 smaller ones (total capacity at least 6 quarts) and spread the stuffing evenly over the bottom. Cover with chicken, then the ground giblets. Pour the sauce over the top and sprinkle lightly with the crumb-and-skin mixture. (You may not need it all.)

9. Bake, uncovered, in a preheated 375° oven 50 to 60 minutes, or until crumbs and sauce are golden and chicken is piping hot. (If baking on two levels, switch casseroles halfway through baking to brown evenly.)

PRESENTATION: Let stand at room temperature 15 to 20 minutes, to cool somewhat. It is best served warm, not piping hot. Sprinkle with chopped parsley and serve directly from casseroles.

To prepare in advance: Complete steps 1 through 8, up to baking the casseroles. Cool and refrigerate, covered, but bring to room temperature before baking.

Note: For such a lengthy recipe it is advisable to cook the chicken one day; to prepare the stuffing and sauce, and assemble, the next; then bake the following day.

Sautéed Watercress

Watercress should not be saved for garnish or salad alone; it is delicious sautéed and served hot. Quick and easy.
May be partially prepared in advance.

> 5 bunches watercress (about 2 pounds)
> 4 tablespoons peanut oil
> 1 teaspoon salt (scant)
> 1½ tablespoons lemon juice

1. Rinse the watercress, drain and cut across in thirds. Store stems and leaves separately, wrapped in towels to absorb remaining moisture.
2. Heat a large skillet or heavy saucepan over high heat. Add the oil and salt; when very hot, add the watercress stems only; sauté, stirring, over high heat until stems turn a deeper green, about ½ minute. Add the watercress leaves and sprinkle with the lemon juice. Stir 2 or 3 more times, then turn out into a heated bowl. The watercress should be tender and only slightly wilted.

PRESENTATION: Serve immediately while hot.

To prepare in advance: Complete step 1, up to sautéing the watercress.

Celériac Rémoulade

Celery root, or celeriac or celery knob, as it is sometimes known, is a root vegetable of the celery family. Prepared in the following manner, it is often listed in the hors d'oeuvre section of a French menu. The vegetable is available in winter. Substitute Celery Leaf Salad (see Index I) when out of season (the recipe should be doubled). Here Celériac Rémoulade is served on a platter with sliced tomatoes garnished with sieved egg.

Must be prepared in advance.

    2 pounds celery root (3 or 4 roots)
    ½ cup white vinegar
    ¼ cup cold water
    1 tablespoon salt
    3 tablespoons Dijon mustard
    1 tablespoon lemon juice
    1 ½ cups Blender Mayonnaise (see Index II)

GARNISH:
Minced parsley

1. Wash celery roots and cut off tops. Peel and drop in cold, salted water (1 teaspoon to 1 quart). Quarter and cut into fine julienne strips (⅛ by ⅛ by 2 inches). Return to salted water as cut to prevent browning, then drain.

2. Combine white vinegar, the ¼ cup cold water and 1 tablespoon salt in a large mixing bowl; add celery root. Let stand 15 minutes to soften and remove some of the bitter flavor. Rinse and dry on paper toweling.

3. In a small bowl beat the mustard and lemon juice with a fork. Gradually stir in the mayonnaise.

4. Pour the rémoulade sauce over the celery root; mix well and let it marinate at least 2 hours, or overnight, refrigerated. For best flavor, serve at a cool room temperature. Yield: about 1 ½ quarts.

PRESENTATION: Serve on platter with tomatoes as directed under *Presentation* for Sliced Tomatoes with Sieved Egg Garnish (below).

SLICED TOMATOES WITH SIEVED EGG GARNISH

May be partially prepared in advance.

> 8 firm, medium tomatoes
> ½ cup olive oil
> 3 tablespoons red wine vinegar
> ½ teaspoon salt
>
> GARNISH:
> 3 hard-cooked egg yolks (see Index II)

1. Chill tomatoes thoroughly before removing skins.
2. Lower tomatoes, 2 at a time, into boiling water for 10 seconds, or until skins loosen. Do not let them "cook" (the chilling will help avoid this). Place in cold water immediately, then remove cores and skin with a small paring knife; the skins should slip off easily if properly blanched.
3. Slice tomatoes across into thick slices; chill.
4. To make the dressing, combine oil, vinegar and salt.

To prepare in advance: Complete all steps except step 3 (skin tomatoes, but do not slice). Refrigerate.

PRESENTATION: Arrange tomatoes, overlapping slightly, around the edge of a large oval platter; salt lightly. Dribble dressing over the top. Press egg yolks through a sieve to garnish tomatoes generously. Spoon Celériac Rémoulade in the center, sprinkle with parsley. Guests should help themselves to a little of each.

Crème de Menthe Torte

Few spectacular desserts are made with as little effort as this one. It is a combination of crème de menthe, melted marshmallows and whipped cream molded in a springform pan lined with ladyfingers. A layer of whipped cream is spread on top and garnished with professional-looking chocolate scrolls you make yourself.

Must be prepared in advance.

  90 to 95 large marshmallows (1 pound, 2 ounces)
  ¾ cup green crème de menthe
   2 pints heavy cream
  22 ladyfingers (about) (3-inch size)

GARNISH:
Chocolate Scrolls (method below)

1. Melt the marshmallows with the crème de menthe in a large saucepan over very low heat, stirring occasionally. Do not allow it to boil. When melted, remove from heat and cool.

2. Whip heavy cream until it mounds lightly (not stiff). Remove 2 cups and reserve for topping. Pour cooled marshmallow mixture over the remainder and fold in until completely distributed.

3. Arrange ladyfingers vertically around the sides of a 9-inch springform pan, sugar side next to the metal. (They will stand better if not separated.)

4. Pour filling into lined springform pan. Spread the reserved whipped cream over the top and garnish with Chocolate Scrolls. Seal with plastic wrap and refrigerate at least 6 hours or until set (overnight is better).

PRESENTATION: Remove rim from springform pan. Place torte on serving tray and present to guests before cutting into wedges. (It cuts easily and holds its shape well.)

Chocolate Scrolls: Let a square of semisweet chocolate stand in a warm place until warm. (An unlit oven is ideal.) Draw a vegetable peeler carefully across the large flat side. The chocolate will come off in curls. (If not, it isn't soft enough.) Do this over a dinner plate and let stand a few minutes until hardened enough for handling. Lift with a spatula and scatter over the torte.

Indexes

I. General Index

A bullet (·) in front of a recipe indicates it is Quick and Easy: that is, the recipe requires little preparation, or can be made at the last minute (sometimes both).

Page numbers in italics refer to the menu in which the recipe appears.

Almond(s): to blanch, 160, 207; to halve, 160; to toast and store, 94
  on Cinnamon Cheesecake, 159–160
  Sauce (for pressed duck), 93–94
  Toasted Chopped (garnish for pressed duck), 94
  · Turkish (for 16), *205*, 207–08
· Ambrosia (for 4), *34*, 42–43
American regional recipes: *see* Index III
Anchovy(ies):
  Butter, Fresh Asparagus with (for 8), *114*, 117–18
  in Stuffed Mushrooms, 82
Anglaise, Sauce (for chocolate Marquise), 223–24
Antipasto, Hot Mixed (for 6), *80*, 80–82
Appetizers (cold):
  · Avocado on the Half Shell with Jellied Consommé (for 6), *63*, 63–64
  · Champignons and Cheese (for 10), *153*, 153–54
  · Cherry Tomatoes (for *gougère*), 163
  Colorful Canapés (for 16), *205*, 205–07
  Curry Peas, *141*, 143
  Eggplant Caviar (for 8), *122*, 122–23
  Four Canapé Pies (for 16), *214*, 214–15

Appetizers (cold) (*cont.*)
  Fresh Artichoke Appetizer (for 10), *141*, 141–42
  Ham Mousse Ardennes (for 8), *114*, 114–15
  Iced Mussels Ravigote (for 4), *44*, 44–46
  · Jellied Consommé, Cream and Caviar (for 6), *90*, 90–91
  Onion Rounds with Parsley Edge (for 16), *225*, 226–28
  Pâté de Foie Liégeois (for 16), *225*, 225–26
  Pickled Shrimp, Texas Style (for 12), *173*, 173–75
  · Roquefort Salad (for 8), *103*, 103–04
  · Taramasalata (for 12), *183*, 183–84
  · Turkish Almonds, *205*, 207–08
Appetizers (hot):
  Fresh Clam Coquilles (for 12), *193*, 193–95
  Gougère, a Burgundian Pastry (for 10), *161*, 161–63
  · Hot Artichoke Appetizers (for 12), *183*, 184–85
  Hot Mixed Antipasto (for 6), *80*, 80–82
  Indian Samosas (for 4), *34*, 34–37
  Shrimp Tempura (for 4), *52*, 52–54
  · Smoked Oyster Canapés (for 8), *122*, 123–24
Apple Shortcake, Swedish (for 6), *63*, 68–69

II. Basic Recipes and Techniques

III. Foreign and American Regional Recipes

BARBARA MYERS, a native of Peoria, Illinois, studied Fine
Arts at Bradley University. After graduating she worked in adver-
tising in Peoria, then for a weekly entertainment guide in Columbus,
Ohio. In 1953 she became the Food Editor of the Columbus Dispatch,
a position which she held for six years.

Since leaving the Dispatch she has pursued her interest in food and
cooking. She has traveled around the world and has focused her at-
tention on the foods of Europe (especially France and Belgium),
Asia and Africa. With her husband, a university professor, and her
daughter, now twelve, she lived for a year in Lima, Peru, and for
eighteen months in Nairobi, Kenya. The manuscript for Invitation to
Dinner was in preparation throughout this period of traveling.